# Mystery without Rhyme or Reason

Laura,
With gratitude!
Enjoy the Mystery!
Michael Coffey

# Mystery without Rhyme or Reason

## Poetic Reflections on the Revised Common Lectionary

MICHAEL COFFEY

Foreword by Walter Brueggemann

RESOURCE *Publications* · Eugene, Oregon

MYSTERY WITHOUT RHYME OR REASON
Poetic Reflections on the Revised Common Lectionary

Resource Publications
An Imprint of Wipf and Stock Publishers
199 W. 8th Ave., Suite 3
Eugene, OR 97401

www.wipfandstock.com

ISBN 13: 978-1-4982-2090-3

Manufactured in the U.S.A.

For Kathryn, Colin, and Liam
my epiphanies, my signs and wonders


With many thanks to Dale Griffith


With deep gratitude to Walter Brueggemann

# Contents

*Foreword*  ix

*Introduction*  xi

Lectionary Year A  1

Lectionary Year B  53

Lectionary Year C  117

*Title Index*  187

*Scripture Index*  191

*Liturgical Index*  195

# Foreword

I HAVE NOT READ anything in a very long time that so amused me, astonished me, convicted me and satisfied me. I had such an experience in reading Michael Coffey's compelling words that I had to find (for me) a new word to characterize it. The word is "quotidian"! It means simply "commonplace, ordinary, routine." That is what his work is: quotidian! It speaks of the concrete, the specific, the most specific, the stuff right in front of us. We hear about food and sleep and bathrobes and grasshoppers and breakfast, the daily stuff that constitutes our life.

For that reason, this poetic exposition should be familiar and commonplace. But of course it is anything but that because Michael has mobilized his pastoral imagination and has transposed ordinary and familiar texts into disclosures that are indeed revelatory. The result is that every text on which he comments takes on a fresh dimension, and a new angle about which I had not thought before. There are those among us who think that the faith attested in the Bible is too old-fashioned, too predictable, too rigorous, or too out of touch to grab attention in a world of rush. But Michael shows otherwise in his words that violate all of our preconceptions in showing us the surprise that awaits us in the text.

At work here is the daring sensibility of a poet who twists and turns us to a new angle. But also at work here is a pastoral theologian who is so well grounded in the tradition that he can explore and probe with ease and with confidence. While so much conventional faith is busy restricting, confining, and limiting, Michael keeps offering new vistas for us and drawing us out beyond where we are. When the lines end, the world is different and the earth has moved under our feet.

My favorite is God's "bathrobe," a riff on the divine "train" that follows God's holiness in the temple vision of Isaiah 6 that frills the entire space. That "train" (now read as "bathrobe"), by the time Michael finishes, fills the entire earth and puts down holy presence here and there well beyond the temple, Michael leads us to wonder why God has on a bathrobe. Perhaps it is Sabbath for coziness for God. Perhaps God had just been through the chaotic waters that were tamed for a bath. Perhaps God is wanting to decode and demystify the high liturgy of the temple, making it less formal and more accessible. I do not know why and Michael does not tell us why. But I do know that I will never read the text of the temple vision with its three-times "holy" the same way again. Nor will the earth ever be the same again, because it is now seen to be God-occupied; the evidence of the divine bathrobe is everywhere, once the poet shows us how to look.

Michael refuses to let us know for sure what the text might mean; he gives us probes, not arguments or explanations or conclusions. The text, in his hands, will not sit still long enough to have "one meaning." His words are not unlike Pentecost. Indeed it is Pentecost every time . . . many tongues, many images, many possibilities that set us off in new freedom. We may be grateful for the tongues in which Michael speaks and writes. This is indeed practical theology as a great form of art. It refuses to dispel the mystery; rather it works to enhance and deepen the mystery of divine presence and purpose by showing us that in the mundane and the quotidian the reality of God comes "bodied" in ways we can handle and parse. When we finish one of his daring testimonies, we need time to linger and reflect and receive. We are surprised at a cognitive level. But in an affective way we are transformed. The Fourth Gospel concludes, "These things are written in order that you may believe . . ." (John 20:31). Surely that is why Michael has taken such great care to get it right. He writes his poetic abundance in order to generate faith, that is, "that we may believe." But the believing to which he invites us is not conventional. He rather hopes that faith will come alive among us in daring, irreverent, impish ways, that the world may be kept open for the coming of Messiah. The cunning with which Michael addresses us corresponds to the cunning of the Gospel narratives themselves. We have learned all too well to flatten out that gospel cunning by dogma and by criticism in order to make it manageable. Michael refuses that and invites us to refuse as well. The alternative to "managing" is hosting and nurturing the words as they work on us. The world around is now mostly explained, controlled, and managed. But it does not give life. What will give life is the word that opens and astonishes and heals. That sort of word is what Michael utters here, for which we may be attentively grateful.

Walter Brueggemann

March 4, 2015, Columbia Theological Seminary

# Introduction

I BEGAN THIS PROJECT as a New Year's resolution. I decided to begin writing a weekly reflection on the lectionary texts used in worship by the majority of churches. I intended to do this for one year. The year came and went and I realized that reflecting poetically on the lectionary texts each week had become a part of my regular spiritual and homiletical discipline. So I kept writing each week, and before I knew it I was completing a set of writings on most Sundays and holy days for the whole three-year Revised Common Lectionary.

It may not seem obvious as first, but this collection of poems is a work of theology. It is obviously not a work of systematic theology, nor is it an exercise in expressing the orthodox tradition of the church through poetry. You might summarize what my own theological leanings and convictions are from these pieces, looking for patterns, common vocabulary, and emphases. But it is not anything close to a *summa theologica*; in some ways the intention of these writings is just the opposite. It is at best a *poetica theologica*.

I have become convinced that the Western theological tradition, as wonderful and insightful as it has been, became too enamored of rational and systematic thought as the sole means of accessing the truth of God. Somewhere along the way, Christians, especially of the academic and clerical type, assumed that the truth of God and our lives was mostly, or even only, captured through rational, intellectual, systematic, and dogmatic writings. All the while, of course, the West continued to produce great visual, written, and musical art, all of which expressed essential truths about God and Christian life, but these expressions of faith and theology have always been relegated a second or third level of importance and truth when it comes to theology.

My conviction is the church would be served well by more poetry, as well as more art and more artists. Walter Brueggemann's book *Finally*

*Comes the Poet* speaks of Isaiah as the prophetic poet who brings poetic truth to a prose-flattened world. His work has greatly influenced my understanding of poetry as a vehicle of theological truth and encounter, seen wonderfully in Isaiah and Jeremiah and Jesus and so much of the great biblical tradition, not to mention the best of the liturgical and ritual traditions of the church. The key point I derive from Brueggemann's phrase here is that poetic truth is not flat. It is not easily resolved into precise statements. It is irreducible and therefore engages the reader, much like so many biblical texts, in a conversation about the truth of God and the world and ourselves, a conversation that is open-ended and never finished.

This, of course, is precisely why poetic expressions of faith and theology are so suited to the task. The One of whom we speak and to whom we speak and listen is not flat, not resolvable, and is irreducible. Therefore, we cannot speak of God in such a way that misleads us into assuming we have captured and controlled God, and so we are finished with God. Poetry, much like humor, is never served well by being explained, but only by being encountered and experienced and confronted by and enjoyed. The same could be said of God.

The word "mystery" is so useful here because it leads us to encounter the holy as something knowable but never fully known or explained. Mystery is something to be enjoyed and experienced, but not explained, at least not in any final, dogmatic way. It is the truth of things that cannot be approached directly, but only sideways, tangentially, with peripheral vision at best.

These poems are, I hope, a way of enjoying the mystery and wrestling with it a bit, and it with us. It is not an attempt to use reason to capture God, but to move beyond reason as the primary category of truth. It is poetry without rhyme or reason, and therefore, maybe in the smallest and most humbling of ways, worthy of its subject.

A note on names for liturgical days: For Sundays outside of particular seasons like Advent or Lent, I am using the designations found in *Evangelical Lutheran Worship*. These days are called, for example, "Lectionary 23 A," and correspond to the "Ordinary" days as named in the Roman Catholic and other lectionaries. The number scheme corresponds to the "Proper" designation by subtracting five. For example, "Lectionary 23 A" corresponds to "Proper 18 A."

# Lectionary Year A

# Hope Is a Blue Note

*Advent 1 A*
Isaiah 2:1–5

*O house of Jacob, come, let us walk in the light of the LORD! (Isa 2:5)*

Hope is a blue note on a jazz-worn clarinet
a chromatic piano chord dissonant and handsome
a minor modal song sung diaphragmatically strong
a silence between hymn and homiletic
puzzling it holds the day in a miter-cornered frame
setting off the eyes of the hopeful like sapphires
a run-on sentence waiting
for some punctuation to signify an end or a pause
or an unknowing or an exclamation of what is yet to come
that is better or more beautiful or at least makes what is now
worth the long, melodic, sorrowful, endless wait

# This Advent

*Advent 2 A*
Isaiah 11:1–10

*A shoot shall come out from the stump of Jesse, and a branch shall grow
out of his roots. (Isa 11:1)*

You light candles and you wait,
not like waiting at the bus stop
with the rain soaking your day
and the time passing like tree growth.

You light candles and you wait,
not like standing in line at the grocery store
with your parsley dripping on your shoe
and the woman in front of you
writing a check like a novel.

You light candles
as you sings songs of joy in minor keys,
and you wait
like a man sitting at the restaurant table
with the calla lilies in hand
and the diamond ring inside
the death-by-chocolate dessert,
looking every direction every moment
to see his beloved appear.
You wait like this
even without anyone coming
to take your flowers,

year after year
war after war
death after death,
lighting candles one by one.

# Quiet Dismissal

*Advent 4 A*
Matthew 1:18–25

> *Now the birth of Jesus the Messiah took place in this way. When his mother Mary had been engaged to Joseph, but before they lived together, she was found to be with child from the Holy Spirit. Her husband Joseph, being a righteous man and unwilling to expose her to public disgrace, planned to dismiss her quietly. (Matt 1:18–19)*

Quiet dismissal is what we do to you
when you are close,
because you flush our faces red
with your pregnant unexpectedness,
invading our strategies and medicaments,
ruining our safe careers and nest-egg certainties.

We would have you sent off Joseph-like
to a small town halfway house clapboard grey
where you can birth your ways behind windows
inaudible, isolated, and irrelevant,
and we can move on to another love and another.

So what singing angel will come to us in reverie
to save us from ourselves and our best intentions,
head off our ego-preserving diplomacies,
and gospel us with the message we dread
and always in need of in our sterile barrenness?

# Sympathy for the Emperor at Christmastime

*Nativity of Our Lord / Christmas Eve*
Luke 2:1–20

> *In those days a decree went out from Emperor Augustus that all the world should be registered. This was the first registration and was taken while Quirinius was governor of Syria. All went to their own towns to be registered. (Luke 2:1–3)*

The outbreak of newness was contagious as a song
containment was unmanageable
even with the emperor's stranglehold of peace

The first case was reported in a barn where
people and domesticated animals share germs
and misery and hunger and cold and labor

From there it was thought to spread to a small band
of sheep herders and a rustic village pub where
they drank pints and harmonized, that may have been where

the traveler was infected with the joy virus
and spread it upstate to an unsuspecting pessimist
who took drugs at first to quell the unusual feeling

From there no one is sure how it became global
other than the emperor and all inoculated like him
did their royal best to spin the good news

birthed that night, but the more they suppressed
the more it lifted up, the more they schemed
the more the glad spirit frustrated their ways

so that anywhere the ease of God disrupts dis-ease,
birth pangs of faith and love and mercy have their way
and people sing and someone catches it

# The Meaning of God

*Christmas 2 ABC*
John 1:1–18

> *And the Word became flesh and lived among us, and we have seen his*
> *glory, the glory as of a father's only son, full of grace and truth.*
> *(John 1:14)*

You wish it could be put into words and paragraphs
recited and parsed and memorized and philosophized
offset printed in a leather-bound book
closed and shelved and dusted for good company

But Logos, Sophia, meaning, divine reason
come to us through the cosmic entanglement
of body and God, with birth pangs and dying pains
and all the light and love you can squeeze in between

so that the meaning of God—
if there ever could be such a thing for us to comprehend—

lives in created flesh and blood and heart and mind
suffers mercy without explanation or cause
births hope without limits or permission
delights in life for all its holy humanity

# Openings and Obfuscations

*Baptism of Our Lord A*
Matthew 3:13–17

> *And when Jesus had been baptized, just as he came up from the water,*
> *suddenly the heavens were opened to him and he saw the Spirit of God*
> *descending like a dove and alighting on him. And a voice from heaven*
> *said, "This is my Son, the Beloved, with whom I am well pleased."*
> *(Matt 3:16–17)*

A break in the clouds split the God-barrier open
the heavens sang and summoned him as benevolence
but then, as always happens and must happen,
the closing, the occlusion of the space between

Whether Jesus' baptism or your own plunging initiation,
perhaps a mystical desert epiphany of dazzling diamond light,
a Himalayan climb into oxygen-starved euphoric heights,
or a canyon ramble descending to depth and profundity,
whether pharmaceutical prescriptions for bliss and dreamland
or wild fungus visions of you outside yourself in glory

You will always re-enter your mundane moment—
like Jesus walking on from the Jordan to middling towns—
you trod again the profane path of normalcy: a breakfast egg,
a morning kiss, money spent, ICU waiting room, neat whiskey,
forest walks, a desk and its chair, all so thick with obfuscation
yet the wonder of it all

# Unbearable Lightness of Myself

*Lectionary 2 A*
Isaiah 49:1–7

*And now the LORD says, who formed me in the womb to be his servant,*
*to bring Jacob back to him, and that Israel might be gathered to him,*
*for I am honored in the sight of the LORD, and my God has become my*
*strength—he says, "It is too light a thing that you should be my servant*
*to raise up the tribes of Jacob and to restore the survivors of Israel; I will*
*give you as a light to the nations, that my salvation may reach to the end*
*of the earth." (Isa 49:5–6)*

He walked into the church office with laptop and lunch bag,
set the coffee mug and stale scone on the desk alongside his Bible,
Scotch tape, and notes from phone calls never returned.

He Tweeted and emailed until his fingers floated off the home keys,
his hair beginning to lift with static electricity,
his feet rising from the blue carpet, his whole body feeling
as if it would soon press against the ceiling fan and hot lights,
his whole life a series of sneaked Wonka Fizzy Lifting Drinks
leaving him too light, lacking substance,

eventually he would float off to the cirrostratus clouds and disappear
beyond the exosphere and Neptune and unnamed constellations
and the event horizon, he would evaporate from memory
not even his dog would miss him.

And then the phone rings and the girl with the unexpected pregnancy
and the ninety-eight year old woman dying alone
and the light bulbs need replacing
before the hungry come to shop the pantry shelves

and the assembling again in the sanctuary where life
once more becomes humble, heavy enough with the holiness
required for there to be visible glory, the thick abiding presence
that holds us beloved on the sun-lit earth.

# Chef

*Lectionary 5 A*
Matthew 5:13–20

*You are the salt of the earth; but if salt has lost its taste, how can its salti-
ness be restored? It is no longer good for anything, but is thrown out and
trampled under foot. (Matt 5:13)*

There is white onion chopping to be done and crying with it
and juliennes of jicama to slice and a slip and a cut and
the vinaigrette must be whisked and emulsified and tested,
balancing of sweet and vinegar to please the palate,
the steak is seared in the black iron pan and peppered
the potatoes roasted in rosemary and garlic browned.

Then the chef does his effortless enchanted toss with salt
delights the tongue and the soul,
taking us back when salt is what we swam in and breathed and sang
so much us that we did not know or taste until we left it.

So it is with God and each other and the love we walked away from.
Now with generous offering we are salted and relished,
offered a taste of love in a bland and hungry world
needing a mere amuse-bouche of the holy we are swimming in.

# Outside Inside Out

*Lectionary 6 A*
Matthew 5:21–37

> *You have heard that it was said to those of ancient times, 'You shall*
> *not murder'; and 'whoever murders shall be liable to judgment.' But I*
> *say to you that if you are angry with a brother or sister, you will be liable*
> *to judgment; and if you insult a brother or sister, you will be liable to the*
> *council; and if you say, 'You fool,' you will be liable to the hell*
> *of fire. (Matt 5:21–22)*

Outside even God he would entreat
with his shirt pressed and untucked
dark jeans carefully faded on the thigh
vanity glasses rightly matching his square face
cheerful humor at the right social moment
generous to friends and strangers with and without
breaking only the smallest of commandments
and rules of engagement on the street and at work.

Inside he knew the heft of carrying like sacked concrete
his own lonesome soul, wretched and loathsome,
a prisoner yoked to his rage and anger,
the deep cavernous drip, drip of fear on stalagmites of terror

now outside God entreating him with compassion untucked,
inside peace rightly matching his wounded heart.

# Edges

*Lectionary 7 A*
Leviticus 19:1–2, 9–18

*When you reap the harvest of your land, you shall not reap to the very
edges of your field, or gather the gleanings of your harvest. You shall not
strip your vineyard bare, or gather the fallen grapes of your vineyard;
you shall leave them for the poor and the alien: I am the LORD your
God. (Lev 19:9–10)*

He farmed the borrowed land like an artisan
caring for nematodes and seedlings and
the soil itself, the nurse of all life.

He harvested with a jeweler's eye each gem of food
feeding family and strangers in village mud cottages
except at the edges he left a row or two along the fence

by the road where wayfarers and immigrants
could pluck and eat and praise
just as he and all do to glorify the soil's maker.

One night he dreamed of the future:
mechanized efficiency, vast acres of
monocultured crops and infertile soil

and he woke with a night terror when he saw
the edges were culled clean and nothing left,
no rough meal for anyone walking by needful.

Sweat and scream filled the bed at the thought,
a godless day and place where no one remembered
edges are where holiness is waiting to be revealed.

# Devouring Fire

*Transfiguration A*
Exodus 24:12–18

> *Now the appearance of the glory of the LORD was like a devouring fire*
> *on the top of the mountain in the sight of the people of Israel.*
> *(Exod 24:17)*

You in your holiness burn hot and wild
and we cannot even touch the fringe
like the sun we can only scuttle our ships
lest we rocket too close and get pulled in

But from time to time and place to place
you let your devouring fire flame free
and in grace it does not burn or consume us
and we can stand to be in your corona unshielded

Moses in the clouds and ocean floors undiscovered
Jesus and Elijah mountaintops and firstborns swaddled
astonishing enactments on earth of your will good and just
moments when the second hand stops and joy lingers

We would grasp you in these moments if we could
but your flames elude our fingers and palms and minds,
our categories and rules, and so you are free
from our control and we are unscorched and glad to be

# Gracious Ritual of Ashes

*Ash Wednesday*
Joel 2:1–2, 12–17

> *Yet even now, says the LORD, return to me with all your heart, with*
> *fasting, with weeping, and with mourning; (Joel 2:12)*

Mark me as one who will not outlast the earth
or the melting icebergs or even the Brooklyn Bridge

Mark me as one who will have a short skip and hop
and reach the end of the sidewalk before too long now

Mark me as one who knows well his nanometric life
and sees in this ephemeral existence a hidden holy gift

Mark me as ash and dust scattered about by artistic wind
landing on a timeless canvas, painting I know not what

# Adam and Eve Again

*Lent 1 A*
Genesis 2:15–17, 3:1–7

*Then the eyes of both were opened, and they knew that they were naked;*
*and they sewed fig leaves together and made loincloths for themselves.*
*(Gen 3:7)*

We can gather at that coffee shop you love
and after a currant scone and a second cup
I can say to you: I'll be Adam, and you can be Eve
and we'll run naked through the orchard free

We can relish our innocence fresh and unaware
as we pluck berries and sit sunlit, grass on skin
discovering again what our bodies are made for
and why we love being just ourselves so

I can follow a slick snake down the unbeaten path
and you can stop and listen to his cues and queries
we can follow him to the tree of knowing
and eat and slurp the juice from our lips and chins

Then we can know and know that we know
and we can cover up and blush and hide ourselves
from our true selves, from the holy within and without
we stumble and fall, lose the gate key and walk on

Later, when grace appears and envelops us
we give thanks that we failed
and knowing we failed, we celebrate becoming,
the letting go of having been

Next morning we rise and walk out fully dressed
we gather at the café, smiling at our hidden nude selves
and I say to you: I'll be Adam, and you can be Eve
and you nod and sip and off we go into the day

# Airstream

*Lent 2 A*
John 3:1–17

*The wind blows where it chooses, and you hear the sound of it, but you
do not know where it comes from or where it goes. So it is with everyone
who is born of the Spirit. (John 3:8)*

Be born of wind and water said the Teacher in the night
be new and swim and soar in the mystery of God now

so Nick polished his Airstream, took it out on the road
from Palo Duro Canyon to Big Bend and beyond

he deleted entries in his Google calendar, went offline
checked off incomplete tasks on his lists driving free

stopping where ever it seemed the flow was flowing
encountering strangers with deep pools of eyes

from time to time someone on the roadside
needed a tire change or a gallon of gas so he stopped

occasionally he met someone at a Waffle House
who sat alone, struck up a conversation, paid the tab

once he met a woman with a thin three-year old and
gave her a year's worth of grocery money just like that

then he stopped and stayed a while in Death Valley heat
drank mango iced tea, absorbed desert wisdom like the sun

when he realized the tires were shot, trip was done,
he gave thanks for that day he trusted the Teacher and took off

gave thanks for letting go, for the restless spirit
moving him fluid through life like wild water streams

# Aquavit

*Lent 3 A*
John 4:5–42

*Jesus answered her, "If you knew the gift of God, and who it is that is say-*
*ing to you, 'Give me a drink,' you would have asked him, and he would*
*have given you living water." (John 4:10)*

If it's true as you say, O abstruse teacher
that you are the pale straw aquavit that we pour
at Christmas and Easter and all the great feasts

Then you infuse us like caraway and cardamom
warm us like whiskey in November
tipsy our imaginations to see you even now

Then how crazy was she at the well to dip and draw
when you stood there like a ribbon wrapped bottle
all gift and wonder, no tax or debit required

How crazy are we like grumpy teetotalers
not to pour a glass and sip with you when
we keep dropping our buckets in empty wells

# If Jesus Were Blind

*Lent 4 A*
John 9:1–41

*Jesus said, "I came into this world for judgment so that those who do not
see may see, and those who do see may become blind." (John 9:39)*

On his face there were only closed lids and not even
the sun could penetrate his corneas with blood red light
but on his fingers he had eyes one on each tip
he could see and feel the world the wind and you

With ten oculi he could peer into the eleventh dimension
see beyond dodecahedrons and hypercubes and superstrings
look into a world our stereoscopic minds cannot envision
he saw the glory beneath the light and within and beyond it

He only saw ultraviolet and infrared, the hidden beauty of things
what hummingbirds see as they hover and zoom and spy
firebush and honeysuckle, sage and yellow trumpet bush
discovering the nectar guides and their honeyed revelations

beyond faces and minds and egos manifested
when he touched you and grasped you inside and out he saw
the you lit up beneath the shadow you, he saw the gash
in your wounded soul, the sweetness dripping from your floral heart

# Sympathy for Lazarus

*Lent 5 A*
John 11:1–45

*Jesus began to weep. So the Jews said, "See how he loved him!" But some
of them said, "Could not he who opened the eyes of the blind man have
kept this man from dying?" (John 11:35–37)*

He didn't ask to be a magic trick like some dead rabbit
pulled out of a stone hat with a hocus pocus incantation.

He didn't want to be resuscitated in full decrepit stink
for his mother to see him shambling down the cemetery road.

He was resting in peace after taking the dark plunge once;
no one should stomach it twice, that long black falling.

So Jesus, when I die and I'm put down to earthen solace
or after my ashes are scattered into entropic chaos irreversible,

do not force me to go through it again like brother Lazarus
raised to face more time in suffering and second death.

Let your tears be so you may let me go as we all must do;
grieve your best friend fully and without recourse to power.

Raise me then beyond time to your un-nameable dimension
where decay has died and all fear of losing myself and you

has been buried in that old entombed world where I still walk
like Lazarus already dead yet alive and yet to die and rise.

# Kenosis

*Palm Sunday / Passion Sunday*
Philippians 2:5–11

> *Let the same mind be in you that was in Christ Jesus, who, though he*
> *was in the form of God, did not regard equality with God as something*
> *to be exploited, but emptied himself, taking the form of a slave, being born*
> *in human likeness. And being found in human form, he humbled himself*
> *and became obedient to the point of death—even death on a cross.*
> (Phil 2:5–8)

My mind so full of debris and hubris from the wasted day,
phone calls unreturned and crumpled scraps of paper,
casual conversations with hidden ego stratifications,
the self I want to project onto a cinema screen large
as a shadow silhouette miming my own celebrated life.

My mind so full like a blue water balloon waiting for
a painful needle prick to burst it open to emptiness
where this small i is no longer my daily migraine throb,
and into my hollow skull a new mind pours like wax
filling every sinus cavity, skull crack and spinal tube.

Your crucified mind so full of hydrangeas and cuttlefish,
the siren of every human voice in full wail and woe,
the birth of stars and the death of orbiting comets,
the faith of the Masai and the death of Western dreams,
the universal background B-flat hum of the holy lover.

Your kenotic mind so full there is no room left for you, and so
freely you let yourself go like a junkie or grey dementia,
until having fallen gorgeously into depravity and death,
the only thing left is for you to be exalted and praised
and your mind to fill mine so in emptiness I am full and free.

# Impatience for Imposters

*Easter 2 A*
John 20:19–31

> *But Thomas (who was called the Twin), one of the twelve, was not with*
> *them when Jesus came. So the other disciples told him, "We have seen*
> *the Lord." But he said to them, "Unless I see the mark of the nails in his*
> *hands, and put my finger in the mark of the nails and my hand in his*
> *side, I will not believe." (John 20:24–25)*

You can walk through walls and do spirit acrobatics
you can come back from a day trip to death
you can haunt us in our daydreams and nightmares

but unless you walk wounded with oxblood scabs
unless you return as once rejected and propagandized
unless you hard code the memory of misery in skin

you are to us only a half-assed matinee magic show
a cheating MacGuffin plot device we groan at and walk out
a Disneyfied ending to a once dark and dense fairy tale

but come to us in your incarnate truth of suffering love
walk with us in our wounded warrior trauma and disease
and we will not only believe but cry my Lord and my God

# New Moon over Emmaus

*Easter 3 A*
Luke 24:13–35

*When he was at the table with them, he took bread, blessed and broke it,
and gave it to them. Then their eyes were opened, and they recognized
him; and he vanished from their sight. (Luke 24:30–31)*

A new moon over Emmaus and in the spacious dark sky
the waning and waxing of an old story forgotten

you know the one where the unfamiliars walk and talk
and share bread and wine and humble deep laughter

where hospitality and conviviality become the norm
and the sacred is tasted and touched in daily routine

where war stories and scar stories are voiced beyond the pain
and the memory of courage eclipses panic and pride

where archetypal hopes of liberation and a world refreshed
rise again like the warming of alcohol in a red cheek flush.

So why is it that just when we get it again, fly-by-night Jesus,
in the breaking and pouring and dining and singing

does it all disappear through a fissure in the evening air
and you wrench us out to find it with some other wayfarer

not just here and now, never settled or fixed in rubrics
we would incant and enact in a Mobius movement nowhere,

but like you, always rising and walking on and out, hungry
for the next meal where strangers become divine companions.

Keep us in phase with your lunatic ways, Jesus of broken bread,
so like the moon we and your wild twilight dream of God

can be new, can sliver some reflection of your light
can spin and orbit and elate into full glow and aura.

# Signs and Wonders

*Easter 4 A*
Acts 2:42–47

*Awe came upon everyone, because many wonders and signs were being
done by the apostles. (Acts 2:43)*


They do not fall like a fireball from the western sky and boom
they do not announce themselves with brass and timpani rolls

while you wait for literal Merlins and alchemists to turn
the dull lead of your life into something prized and shiny

while you wonder if Jesus himself might spit in mud and
make you see or get you up off the invalid matt to dance

signs and wonders happen when people gather in memory
of the one who broke bread and shared it beyond frontiers

the poor are honored, gladness swells like full moon high tide
awe fills dumb-founded souls with mystery secreted in each hour

tears flow from all who are lost in it and cannot explain it
and do not have to, tears of exuberance,

tears of grief, tears for life itself,
this is our sign and our wonder, that we are here at all.

# Show Us

*Easter 5 A*
John 14:1–14

> *Philip said to him, "Lord, show us the Father, and we will be satisfied."*
> *Jesus said to him, "Have I been with you all this time, Philip, and you*
> *still do not know me? Whoever has seen me has seen the Father. How*
> *can you say, 'Show us the Father'?" (John 14:8–9)*

Show us the Father, we prayed, and Jesus
stood before us crazy calm and unkempt
fingers rough from the lathe and chisel, mind
open to absorb all, even us, into compassion.

Show us the Spirit, we chanted in the night,
and the wind exhaled through the sheer curtains
and our hair and confusion. We breathed in
the lively scents of rosemary and desert sage.

Show us the mystery, we hummed, and every
cancer fighter on the globe lit up orange
as dots of fear and courage, and
joy and humility at death beds and healing hands.

Show us the divine we uttered into the universe
and water molecules assembled as a reflecting pool
we stooped and strained, peered long and deep
until we saw not only ourselves, but each other.

# Groping

*Easter 6 A*
Acts 17:22–31

*From one ancestor he made all nations to inhabit the whole earth, and
he allotted the times of their existence and the boundaries of the places
where they would live, so that they would search for God and perhaps
grope for him and find him—though indeed he is not far from each one
of us. For 'In him we live and move and have our being'; as even some of
your own poets have said, 'For we too are his offspring.' (Acts 17:26–28)*

There is somewhere in the murkiness and dusk
that fills in the spaces between the photons
somewhere between strings of nanoseconds
and the fine wire of time holding them in necklace

There is somewhere in the thin pages of the dogmatics
between the Trinity and the Christology and the ink
and fiber paper that forms a lucid notion of God
in your neurons and transmits it to mine and theirs

There is somewhere between the flowing stream
and the sound of the flowing stream and the ear
that receives its gloshing as gift of delight and chaos
and the brook trout that hides silent beneath the current

There is amid the known and the unknown numinous
another who is neither and the same, both more and less
named and unnamed, present and inside of presence
a this and a that for which we grope and never grasp

Kyrie and Gloria call and more than echo answers
it is not the squeezing of the mystery in our arms
that gives this holy life pleasure and purpose but
the feeling of it eternally slipping like silk through our fingers

# Trinity Is a Poem

*Holy Trinity A*
Second Corinthians 13:11–13

> *The grace of the Lord Jesus Christ, the love of God, and the communion of the Holy Spirit be with all of you. (2 Cor 13:13)*

Trinity is a free verse cosmic love gift
sending sound waves through earth to hurl speech
into the ionosphere stirring radio waves to hum

Trinity is a synchronistic dream we and God have
nightly about the interface of human and divine
the matrix of connections between holy and common

Trinity is a syncopated counterpoint of melody lines
referencing each other and making music as sonorous
as whales and pulsars and seismic waves all held in tension

then someone inscribed the free utterance in indelible ink
and someone analyzed the shared dream with Freudian precision
and someone forced the messy melodies smooth in straight time

behold: just when they think they finished the job and
brush the dust of such work off their hands and rest
Trinity dances out the door and finds willing partners to twirl

# Sentinels

*Lectionary 23 A*
Ezekiel 33:7–11

*So you, mortal, I have made a sentinel for the house of Israel; whenever*
*you hear a word from my mouth, you shall give them warning from me.*
*(Ezek 33:7)*

They came to us like sirens across the frothing ocean
we thought it was the sound of death, we thought it trouble
but it was all our own trouble bouncing back at us off sea cliffs
across waves and through wind and by wires

At first we ignored it like your own child's whine
but it kept coming with force and insistence and pressure
until the point came where we saw it clear as a neon sign:
this is the right turn, the chance, the change required

There were beheadings and melting bergs and street riots
a man set himself on fire as he prayed for infinite peace
bees dropped from their hives leaving food crops unfertile
bruised women no longer hid their wounds behind doors or veils

The pain of the universe will keep pulsing the sentinels strong
some folks will intercept and decipher and ponder and act
some will dismiss them like a run-in with a rambling man
who says these are the words of the divine we were waiting for

# Abacus

***Lectionary 24 A***
Matthew 18:21–35

> *Then Peter came and said to him, "Lord, if another member of the*
> *church sins against me, how often should I forgive? As many as seven*
> *times?" Jesus said to him, "Not seven times, but, I tell you, seventy–seven*
> *times. (Matt 18:21–22)*

There was the time you lied about the car crash
and the time I told you I didn't go to the corner bar.

There was the time you let the cat out and she got crushed
and the time I let loose my tongue and spit venom.

This is how we hurt each other: not in the act
but in the clinging and the trumpeting of wounds
and the holding on to justice like a rapier

sliding and clicking the abacus beads for each injury
from the coveting to the stealing and adultering
the killing, the lying, the false accusing and the rest.

As if by keeping tally, and keeping a balance of accounts
we could make our offenses against each other fair
and we end not with balanced books, but endless debt.

Or we could stop the counting and winning
and see how the calculus of grace breaks the abacus

and strings the beads into a polished necklace, gifted to each other
with laughter and humility and freedom and zeroed lines.

# It Was a Good Day for God

*Lectionary 25 A*
Matthew 20:1–16

*Am I not allowed to do what I choose with what belongs to me? Or are you envious because I am generous? (Matt 20:15)*

Before the sundown sip of three-cubed Irish whiskey
and the pondering of the universe and counterpoint
and the choice to give time its particular flow

it titillated the Almighty to place that random
twenty dollar bill on the floor next to the chair
where the college student studied empty-walleted

it gave goose bumps to the Lord's arms to let
the wind loosen the church door latch and the
misplaced woman on the stoop came in for the night

it was a holy thrill to speak absolution to a man who
figured out how to purge all his needle-stick guilt
and put himself in a place of pleading and let it go

a long day for a researcher in communicable disease
ended with a novel idea from nowhere on how
a vaccine might be tweaked for double effectiveness

by dinner the Great One enjoyed inspiring a stuck poet
with the words *bounteousness* and *exultation*
and fingers eager to put fearless words on the page

it was a good day to be God when generosity
was seen as the goodness of God and this
goodness was praised as the Godness of God

# The Third Yes

*Lectionary 26 A*
Matthew 21:23–32

*What do you think? A man had two sons; he went to the first and said,
 'Son, go and work in the vineyard today.' He answered, 'I will not';
 but later he changed his mind and went. The father went to the second
 and said the same; and he answered, 'I go, sir'; but he did not go. Which
 of the two did the will of his father?" They said, "The first."*
(Matt 21:28–31a)

My first yes was eager and earnest and ill-thought
it was spirited and bouncing and saw the whole
world like a Chicago snow globe I could shake into beauty
but I shook nothing and made no magnificence here

My second yes was my ego in search of positioning
and a title and a moment on the dais under lights
so everything I signed up for ended dissonant
and cracked and unfinished like a garage hobby

And then came my honest, exhausted, deflated no
and I merely made my bed and tipped the barista
held the door for the guy with the baby stroller
answered the phone with a helpful thought or two

And then as I held onto no and not me and not now
you uttered the unexpected yes into this slight life of
saving no one and fixing little and mostly walking with
arms and eyes open to the next and tiniest of faithful things

# Architecture

*Lectionary 27 A*
Matthew 21:33–46

*Jesus said to them, "Have you never read in the scriptures: 'The stone
that the builders rejected has become the cornerstone; this was the Lord's
doing, and it is amazing in our eyes'? (Matt 21:42)*

Was it Frank Lloyd Wright who said it was
just as desirable to build a chicken house as it was
a cathedral, and if so did he ever build a coop
that changed the world like the churches of
Falling Water or Robie House or the Guggenheim

my guess is no and so I'd say go for cathedrals
but don't venerate or praise their immaculateness
they are like the building up of your soul or
your self if you could construct your temple self

and then no matter your effort or fortitude or refutation
every stone you select for your self-anointed project
will have a chip or be out of plumb or fissured
and skew every door and archway and spire
just hurting the eyeball enough that you will labor
long days anguishing over the faults and the cracks

your heart will sorrow that you never got it right
this blueprint and fabricating that is you and your
cathedral of St. Perfection, until you are moved

to kiss the stone you rejected, yours and God's,
the mortal flaws and unfinished structural promises,
and to call the chicken house of your ramshackle life
a basilica of the divine, an architecture of the holy

# Ready to Party

*Lectionary 28 A*
Matthew 22:1–14

*But when the king came in to see the guests, he noticed a man there who
was not wearing a wedding robe, and he said to him, 'Friend, how did
you get in here without a wedding robe?' And he was speechless. Then the
king said to the attendants, 'Bind him hand and foot, and throw him into
the outer darkness, where there will be weeping and gnashing of teeth.'
For many are called, but few are chosen. (Matt 22:11–14)*

Your parabolic outer darkness does not scare me off,
O tough and craggy Jesus, who pushes us harder than
milquetoast indulgent Jesus of our adolescent imaginations.

Your vivid stereoscopes of weeping and gnashing teeth
do not intimidate us like some mob threats or politicians
pulling every parliamentary stunt to get what they want.

How can you, Risen One, panic anyone who reads you well
who already knows the weighty black of outer darkness
who has cried all tears to dryness and ground teeth to nubs?

The only thing left is your offer of a white robe at the party door
handed freely to all for the revelry of your love supreme
perhaps with a glass of vintage wine that graces the palate

Only a frozen statue who never suffered would say no I will not,
only a proud man who insisted on life on his own terms shuns it,
only a woman who feared most to be out of style tosses it aside.

But we who have tried life on our own terms for too long,
who suffered every addiction and endless anxious days alone,
we who are already naked wear it gladly to the feast of now.

# Tattoo

*Lectionary 29 A*
Matthew 22:15–21

> *Show me the coin used for the tax." And they brought him a denarius.*
> *Then he said to them, "Whose head is this, and whose title?" They*
> *answered, "The emperor's." Then he said to them, "Give therefore to the*
> *emperor the things that are the emperor's, and to God the things that are*
> *God's." (Matt 22:19–21)*

The unseen artist uses invisible inks and needles them
into you in patterns and colors and words
that work their way beneath the epidermis and dermis
right on through to the blood and the bone
and with electric impulse make their way to
nerve fiber and spine on up to the cerebral cortex
there your holy tattooed brand shapes visions
causes revelations of who and why you are,
notions of what you are inspired to do on this earth
with your body and mind, your money and heart
and seconds slipping by even now you count them down.

Swayed by the indelibility of your own extravagant worth
you resist spending your coins or bills or compassion or vigor
on the shenanigans of market gods and credit seductions;
you repel from falling into the bloated trap of allegiance
to nation or munitions or religious tribe
which will take all you have to give
until you have spent yourself empty
all of you, even the parts you meant to save for yourself.

One marked and signified and summoned such as you
will spend the wealth of yourself as the artist does,
pouring out costly love like blood meal on marigolds
inking life into the art of another expensive soul,
living the artist's dream of a gorgeously colored world
as yet only sketched on the canvas of our marvelous minds.

# Grief on a Hallowed Eve

*All Saints / All Souls*
Revelation 7:9–17

*Then one of the elders addressed me, saying, "Who are these, robed in white, and where have they come from?" I said to him, "Sir, you are the one that knows." Then he said to me, "These are they who have come out of the great ordeal ;they have washed their robes and made them white in the blood of the Lamb. (Rev 7:13–14)*

You'll put it in a music box on the dresser
in the guest room where you only go to dust
or you'll hide it in a milky white vase on the mantel
and not pay it attention when you, sipping wine, light a fire.

But then you'll walk past the guitar with the capo
your grandfather gifted you for no reason in his last year;
the cherry wood dining table that was grandmother's;
you drive by the burger joint where your dad said
you will be magnificent and you already are;
you'll walk on the hardwood floors your
mother said wouldn't they look lovely if refinished
and they are, but not before she died.

And so the grief you carry cannot be hid long
before it jumps out at you,
a skeleton behind the front oak tree on Halloween
before all the saints are remembered.

So just when you thought the day was ordinary and tearless,
all these dead and the fragments of their holy lives
haunt and stir you to imagine your own dying day,
every grief is here to stay, waiting, they just need you
like the dog to take them out and play with them a while
to let them entangle and wrestle and empty you again
so you have room for the dead to rise
and fill you with their wisdom only offered
to those who pause to weep and then
your ghostly beloved and God with them
make your life hallowed again.

# You Are Late

*Lectionary 32 A*
Matthew 25:1–13

*As the bridegroom was delayed, all of them became drowsy and slept.*
*(Matt 25:5)*

And you are late as we wait for the dateless day
the time of no more car crashes or heroin overdoses
the futility of armaments and warlords revealed
the unscheduled happening on the skyline beyond
a joyous enigma warbled by shofar, drum, and didgeridoo
a jubilee table overflowing with peppered roast and pie
every person has a dining chair and every chair a person.

So we wonder, in your holy lateness that feels stale now
as our wicking lamps burn dry and our oil flasks empty
like our fading hope and trust in the thinness of words
did we miss something or was there nothing to miss
did we blink in the wind as you hurriedly came and went
did you forget us or just move on to other universes and
other promises easier to keep than healing this one

or is it that we blithely forgot what we were waiting for and
it is here touching like sunlight fingers and nearby as Mars
round and full of presence like pregnant women waxing
sublime like Grand Canyon silence filling the ear and mind,
is it you yourself and your permeation of every quantum thing
so all we do now in the felt deferment that is not quite that
is welcome you slowly like this day's light one photon after the other.

# Lectionary Year B

# Hidden Face

*Advent 1 B*
Isaiah 63:1–9

> *O that you would tear open the heavens and come down, so that the mountains would quake at your presence. There is no one who calls on your name, or attempts to take hold of you; for you have hidden your face from us, and have delivered us into the hand of our iniquity.*
> *(Isa 64:1, 7)*

Your face wrapped in muslin like an ancient mummy
or a belly dancer concealed in a silky mysterious move

occasionally a peek through the fabric comes at night
and we catch a sliver of an eye or pursed lip and philtrum

you hide your countenance in the warp and woof of time
that barely enough of you will filter through the weave

enough and enough of this game, holy hidden funster
scissor through, poke a hole, tear the drapery down

do not leave us wondering about day and hour
and what and when and war and peace and love

open up to us and delight our hopeful eyes with your beauty
and we might with enough convincing just do the same

# Wild Man John

*Advent 2 B*
Mark 1:1–8

*Now John was clothed with camel's hair, with a leather belt around his
waist, and he ate locusts and wild honey. (Mark 1:6)*

Rough like bark and a bark like a feral December dog
no smooth salesman with a fold out suitcase
his work is black pumice, his words spray forth
like sandblasting, like crystallized winter winds.

He leads us to where no gentleman or clergy could
a ritual place hidden in the woods in the mossy darkness
where our dread trembling shakes off veneers of goodness
we no longer don the icy cool surface of nice and okay

Take us down deep into every damnable thing we hide about us
until our egos crack like eggs and white and yellow spill forth
to incubate in your woolly wildness—some new man who
no longer lives for tame visions but only madcap holy ones.

# Fluo•res•cence

*Advent 3 B*
Isaiah 61:1–4, 8–11

*There was a man sent from God, whose name was John. He came as a witness to testify to the light, so that all might believe through him. He himself was not the light, but he came to testify to the light. (John 1:6–8)*

Fluo•res•cence: the property of absorbing
light of short wavelength and
emitting light of longer wavelength.

The illuminate one radiates love
at frequencies higher than our
blue eyes and red souls can see and so

something ultraviolet is going on
around us and in us and through us
and our molecules quiver and warm

at one time I was young and wanted
to light the world with gospel and
the world would shine like glitter

after twenty years of dim effort
and quavering and rarely a flint spark
I can see how it goes now with us

I am not the light
and this is a gift I receive
like an excised tumor clean

I am not the light
though occasionally I fluoresce
with the love supreme

# No Angel Came

*Advent 4 B*
Luke 1:26–38

*Then Mary said, "Here am I, the servant of the Lord; let it be with me according to your word." Then the angel departed from her. (Luke 1:38)*

She was eight months full and plump
wrapped in a pink faux fur jacket
sat ringless on the front stoop
reading Seventeen for survival

he was listless in bed tucked in
by the gravity of his phobic mind
headphones buffering the noise
of guns and street and mother

unlike timeworn stories of glowing envoys
befuddled virgins unwed
clear signals of holy plans
and playbooks already drawn

no angel came to make good news
of your plot or mollify your pain
no messages fluttered down
from the clouds like ticker tape

so here is your Gabriel with the word
your hushed heart needs from beyond:
fear not, drop shame, stand tall,
carry on, good courage, sing out

you may not be Mary-esque in blue
and embrace your story loud and strong
but something will be birthed from you
and only you can labor it to life for this world

God has chosen you for some essential
tinted dot in the panoramic pointillist canvas
so now let it out, your humble yowl,
your magnifying, audacious, wanton praise

# In the Night

*Nativity of Our Lord / Christmas Eve*
Luke 2:1–20

*And she gave birth to her firstborn son and wrapped him in bands of cloth, and laid him in a manger, because there was no place for them in the inn. (Luke 2:7)*

*A Christmas Song*

In the cold of night
as Mary held her baby tight,
O, warm us, hold us
in your love, God with us, in Christ.

In the lonely night
as Mary calmed her baby's fright,
O, still us, comfort us
in your love, God with us, in Christ.

In the peaceful night
as Mary trusted all was right
O, guide us, hearten us,
with your love, God with us, in Christ.

In the dark of night
as Mary saw her baby's light,
O, shine on, shine on us
with your love, God with us, in Christ.

# Training to See Stars

*Epiphany of Our Lord*
Matthew 2:1–12

> *In the time of King Herod, after Jesus was born in Bethlehem of Judea,*
> *wise men from the East came to Jerusalem, asking, "Where is the child*
> *who has been born king of the Jews? For we observed his star at its rising,*
> *and have come to pay him homage." (Matt 2:1–2)*

It may have been a long course of study over years
books and lectures and experimentation and dissertations
or perhaps it was a week-long seminar at the Hilton in
the ballroom with Persian style carpet and crystal chandeliers.

I suppose it could have been a drugstore pamphlet
picked up on the way to some other happening but
I'm guessing it was more like jiu-jitsu and grappling
and training on the ground with slow accreditation.

But somehow those magi were trained to see the light
and when the light came and no one else comprehended
they were ready and wide-eyed, awestruck and epiphanied
caught up in the journey of life on the holy unmapped road.

And you and I, what training, what discipline and diligence
have we done when we look at the sky in longing and wonder
or in each other's eyes wanting and groping for some twinkling
some swirling Van Gogh star of divine guidance for the passage?

# Melt

*Baptism of Our Lord B*
Genesis 1:1–5

*In the beginning when God created the heavens and the earth, the earth
was a formless void and darkness covered the face of the deep, while a
wind from God swept over the face of the waters. Then God said, "Let
there be light"; and there was light. (Gen 1:1–3)*

When all fine things melt away,
platinum and books and Chagall oils and jazz
and even memory becomes
another drop in the liquid cosmos

there will be, as in the beginning,
a light, an emanating presence permeating darkness,
absorbing all disparate thoughts and persons
into one, and this one you may call Christ,
the story of all that lives, dies, and is renewed.

And when you are one with flowing truth
and love has enveloped you and accepted
you into its infinite pool
where will your beliefs be then?
What utterances of your small mind
and self-satisfied tongue will survive?
What contrivances of the god you
once held firmly in your breast pocket
next to your fountain pen
will you cling to then?

For which inflated mylar balloon of yourself
will you still hold the string?

No, you will gladly, freely,
lovingly let each one flow like water
through your fingers and you will be satisfied
to be a part of what you once
wished to have mere distant, controlling knowledge of.

So why, if this same fluid universe
has baptized you already into your belovedness
and puddled you up with everything and everyone
have you not yet let go and melted,
you fine thing?

# Samuel Sleeping in the Temple

*Lectionary 2 B*
First Samuel 3:1–10

*Then the LORD called, "Samuel! Samuel!" and he said, "Here I am!"*
*(1 Sam 3:4)*

A subversive night voice calls.
It's not who you think.
Run like hell, or say: *yes, me!*

# Have You Not Known, Grasshopper

*Lectionary 5 B*
Isaiah 40:21–31

*Have you not known? Have you not heard? Has it not been told you from the beginning? Have you not understood from the foundations of the earth?*
*It is he who sits above the circle of the earth, and its inhabitants are like grasshoppers; who stretches out the heavens like a curtain, and spreads them like a tent to live in; who brings princes to naught, and makes the rulers of the earth as nothing. (Isa 40:21–23)*

What a relief and what a cause
of humility right down to my exoskeleton.
The shaping of the earth
and the timing of the rains

the rising of the sun
and the spreading of the stars on the sky
the making and crowning of kings
and the dethroning of prideful powers

does not depend on me
a grasshopper in the field of the world.
But the world does depend on me
to hop and nibble on the grass

and stop and take notice with my compound eyes
of the sun, the sky, the muscle and immodesty of kings
and with my mandibles in full song
let praise and protest rise above me.

# When My Time Comes for Ashes and Dust

## Ash Wednesday
Psalm 51:1–17

> *O Lord, open my lips, and my mouth shall proclaim your praise.*
> *(Ps 51:15)*

When my time comes for ashes and dust
and final things said and momentary lament
let there be tears freely flowing in the congregation
and a bit of wailing for a while to get things going

and then let there be in the frankincensed aisles
when the cross makes its way
past the black suits and pressed handkerchiefs
and children fidgeting oblivious to ritualized grief—

let there be a procession of drums stirring the souls
of those who still have heartbeat rhythms,
djembes and doumbeks, tree drums and rattle gourds
calling to the wildness of all the still living and all too tame

downbeats and syncopations
and finger riffs in complicated cadences
and hands red from so much music making
reminding everyone who came for me

in between the silences and the intonation
of the twisting walk through the labyrinth of life
I made some music, loving in time and in counterpoint,
but too tamed when it needed to echo the divine feral call,

the ecstasy song of my paschal stride through the universe.
But you breathers even in grief still have hands, fingers, and hearts
and before your final walk down the aisle in a small ashy urn
you have a dancing pulse urging you to

more wildness and less caution
more drumming and less watching from a distance
more moving in your skin as God moves through you
in this percussive dance around the firelight of infinite love.

# Jesus Naked in a Sacred Circle

*Lent 1 B*
Mark 1:9–15

*And a voice came from heaven, "You are my Son, the Beloved; with you I am well pleased." And the Spirit immediately drove him out into the wilderness. He was in the wilderness forty days, tempted by Satan; and he was with the wild beasts; and the angels waited on him. (Mark 1:11–13)*

You are my beloved son
said the father into his wet ears

as he came up out of Jordan mud water
out of chaos out of death out of yesterday

only to be whooshed off into tomorrow
still dripping, cold-shocked, and gasping

into wilderness where if he survives and is hardened,
if he resists, if he lets go, if he inhales spirit

temptation will come like a pesky fly
and a mere slow hand wave will move it along

and gut growls will teach him to hunger
and parched dry throat to thirst

for all the right things in the right way
and not fear the hunger, the thirst, the teaching

the unfinished business that cannot be perfected
in this life, not in time, not in space, not in body

so I wonder as he sat in his sacred circle naked
and let the wild beasts teach him and holy messengers tend him

did he know the wilderness was only the beginning
and everything after would tempt him all over again

to safety, to comfort, to grasping after certitudes
when God would only offer silence

on the road, in the garden, on the bloody hillside
in the cry, in the abandonment, in the false hope

did he know this during the forty days
or did he imagine he would find an easier path

perhaps work for a down payment on a Nazarene cottage
and whittle toys in the evening by the fire

sitting there whistling an old tune
as a fly lands on his cheek and will not move

# Occupy Temple

*Lent 3 B*
John 2:13–22

*In the temple he found people selling cattle, sheep, and doves, and the
money changers seated at their tables. Making a whip of cords, he drove
all of them out of the temple, both the sheep and the cattle. He also
poured out the coins of the money changers and overturned their tables.
He told those who were selling the doves, "Take these things out of here!
Stop making my Father's house a marketplace!" (John 2:14–16)*

Jesus, you really did it this time
didn't you? You let your dark anger seep
through the pores of your glowing skin

you who flings all gates right off their hinges
granting access to fatherly and motherly divine love
flowing through every cubic inch of air

you turned and tripped and toppled tables
and scattered coins and freed temple doves
and I bet you yelled in a gruff croak:

stop locking up the holy in a box
in a temple, in a creedal subscription, in a poll tax
and let the holy flow uncontrolled like Ezekiel's river

# Sacred Wound Lifted Up

*Lent 4 B*
John 3:14–21

*And just as Moses lifted up the serpent in the wilderness, so must the Son of Man be lifted up, that whoever believes in him may have eternal life.*
*(John 3:14–15)*


God you got me snake bit
and woke me up to the hypodermic fangs
I use to inject my poison into the world,
into my best loving self, into my pained self.
And then in your magnanimous, ironic wit
you put it all on a stick,
lifted it up to the cool blue cloudless sky
and tricked me into looking at my own folly.

When my own wound undressed up there
became my healing deep in here
I winked at your Asclepius' rod,
your cross, your snakey Jesus magic,
and you, you who brings venom and anti-venom,
who heals even when it hurts,
you winked back and I knew I could
shed some skin and slither on.

# What to Do with Your One Grain of Wheat

*Lent 5 B*
John 12:20–30

*Very truly, I tell you, unless a grain of wheat falls into the earth and dies,*
*it remains just a single grain; but if it dies, it bears much fruit.*
*(John 12:24)*

Either way you're gonna die:
clutching your seed in your fist
buried in your Sunday suit
the lid sealed shut with a rubber gasket
watertight lifetime guarantee,
impermeable to the forces of nature.
But the seed sprouts and its pale stem
pushes through your dried fingers
and urges upward straining for sunlight
until it bumps the steely casket lid
and bends and arcs downward finally surrendering.

Either way you're gonna die:
You can open your hand and let loose
the grain of love you bear.
You can open your protected soul
to life and death and mystery in the breathable air.
You can plant your seed in the welcoming earth
and die to your fear and let something uncontrollable grow.
When you are buried like the seed

73

it is already free to break through soil
and let the sun kiss it to life
and sprinkle the earth with a thousand new grains.

Either way you're gonna die:
But if you let your seed go
and die before you die
there will be wheat and flour enough
to bake bread with holy wild yeast
and feed the hungry world,
which gives thanks for your small grain
to the One who made you to die for the fruit of love.

# Passiontide

*Then Jesus gave a loud cry and breathed his last. And the curtain of the temple was torn in two, from top to bottom. Now when the centurion, who stood facing him, saw that in this way he breathed his last, he said, "Truly this man was God's Son!"*

*There were also women looking on from a distance; among them were Mary Magdalene, and Mary the mother of James the younger and of Joses, and Salome. These used to follow him and provided for him when he was in Galilee; and there were many other women who had come up with him to Jerusalem. (Mark 15:37–41)*

And so the time comes to let you go again
like Mary at her weeping station
like Peter in his running shameful cry
like Mary Magdalene's sad watchful eye
like the soldier's gasping epiphany
like Joseph gently laying your body down and releasing you
into the tomb the darkness the empty unknown.

We would rather hang on to you friend
and let Simon take the cross as you slip out of line
catch a taxicab out of town
and escape into your suburban green lawn hideaway
where we drop by for a Sunday cookout and a Bud.
The mosquitoes would hover around us like angels
singing *holy, holy, holy* and smell our breath and sweat

and bite you and draw a blood drop
and we look at each other and we know now
as we hang our weeping heads
that nothing ever gets done in clinging comfort.

And so the time comes to let you go again
and let God do the divine metamorphosis
of every weeping, shameful, sad, gasping, gentle release
into the tomb of darkness where you meet us in emptiness
where when we let you go, we let ourselves go also
as we fall into the earthy black of surrender
and wait, wait, wait for your next creation out of nothing
your unexpected goodness bleeding through.

# The Resurrection Theater of the Absurd

*Resurrection of Our Lord / Easter Sunday B*
Mark 16:1-8

*When the sabbath was over, Mary Magdalene, and Mary the mother of*
*James, and Salome bought spices, so that they might go and anoint him.*
*And very early on the first day of the week, when the sun had risen, they*
*went to the tomb. They had been saying to one another, "Who will roll*
*away the stone for us from the entrance to the tomb?" (Mark 16:1–3)*

You surprised me when you
stepped on my grief and rudely interrupted
my expectations for the show to end

when I assumed we would walk out in darkness
down city streets and go for a martini and talk about
that cross and the dramatic lighting and all that emptiness after

and then we could pick up our heavy heads
and hold them lopsided as we went on our mournful way
living the grey life we always imagined.

But then you, you wizard of astonishment,
you author of unexpected epilogues
you springtime of wildflowers in greened up dead fields

you resurrected my small mind above the predictable plot formulas
and opened up the stone laid over my heart,
so heavy, and yet with you, so easily, so gracefully rolled away.

# We Know Love by This

*Easter 4 B*
First John 3:16–24

*We know love by this, that he laid down his life for us—and we ought to lay down our lives for one another. How does God's love abide in anyone who has the world's goods and sees a brother or sister in need and yet refuses help? Little children, let us love, not in word or speech, but in truth and action. (1 John 3:16–18)*

You tell me you love me like pomegranate
and I take you to the fruiting tree to pluck one

You tell me you love me with silky words
and I spin you thread and weave a shawl to wrap you

You speak to me about romance and what once warmed you
and I chop the wood and kindle the fire

You say you love certain words like *cantaloupe*
and I cube the melon for your breakfast

You tell me love is in the ether and cannot be pointed to
and I frame the house that contains it

You tell me you are dying to love me more but don't know how
and I lay down my life for you so that you can

# Friending

***Easter 6 B***
John 15:9–17

*I do not call you servants any longer, because the servant does not know
what the master is doing; but I have called you friends, because I have
made known to you everything that I have heard from my Father.*
*(John 15:15)*

You friended us, Jesus, and we clicked "like"
and you said meet me Thursday at the Ocotillo Pub

we had a few beers and played darts
and bullshitted about our conquests and glory days

until you told us what your embodied friending
exacts of us, of yourself:

The non-virtual friend lays down real life
like combat buddies on the front line

the one who hurdles to take the bullet
the one who treads the mine field first

or in the battlefield of the warring soul
who listens to the lacerations without flinching

who puts down his smartphone distractions
and removes the taciturn armor of self-protection

who prods your sore spots until you curse
and admit that bandages have not healed

and bro hugs you strong until you both know
you're going to weep on each other's shoulder

and throw another dart or two drinking Trappist brew
hanging out until they say: *last call.*

You're gone now, friend, but we still go to the pub
limping along like Jacob from our old injuries

slaking our thirst in good company, befriending
strangers with gaping wounds, raising a glass to you.

# Ascension

## Ascension of Our Lord
Acts 1:1–11

> *When he had said this, as they were watching, he was lifted up, and a cloud took him out of their sight. (Acts 1:9)*

Where is "up" for you now
that you have slipped from our sight
but still find your way into our being

we have been above the clouds
and planted lunar footprints
and watched Voyager move beyond the heliosphere

all we saw was a vast lonely world
not a trace of your friendly face
not even that visage in the rocks of Mars

So where is "up" for you, anyway?
Is it like a hypercube that we can't construct
in our 3D world, but only see shadows of

or is it a furtive movement within
a shifting expanse in space-time so that you
move beyond the infinite and wormhole your way back to us

and so your up has become a down
into our bodies and minds and heres and nows
and bread and wine and thanksgiving

# Pentecost Spiked Punch

*Day of Pentecost*
Acts 2:1–21

*Indeed, these are not drunk, as you suppose, for it is only nine o'clock in
the morning. No, this is what was spoken through the prophet Joel: 'In the
last days it will be, God declares, that I will pour out my Spirit upon all
flesh, and your sons and your daughters shall prophesy, and your young
men shall see visions, and your old men shall dream dreams.*
*(Acts 2:15-17)*

We are not think like you drunk we are
we are high on a free-pouring spirit

we are not imagine like you confused we are
our minds are cleared now more than before

this is not the feared you nightmare would come true
this is the young man's dream and old woman's beatific vision

this is not the twist and wiggle you enslavement to escape
this is the liberation you never hoped of hoping for

you don't saying what I am know because
the fire has not yet singed your hair off

and exposed your scalp to the holy hurricane blowing on you
and opened you up to the expansive vista of life in the sacred

your eyes are still reading the right words the wrong way
still looking for logic and precision in a fuzzy universe

still listening to echoes of fear and whispers of blame
but even just now something is stirring you to hear again

something is moving among us that makes sense of our nonsense
that make sense no matter which order or language you speak them

# God's Bathrobe

*Holy Trinity*
Isaiah 6:1–8

> *In the year that King Uzziah died, I saw the LORD sitting on a throne, high and lofty; and the hem of his robe filled the temple. Seraphs were in attendance above him; each had six wings: with two they covered their faces, and with two they covered their feet, and with two they flew. And one called to another and said: "Holy, holy, holy is the LORD of hosts; the whole earth is full of his glory." (Isa 6:1–3)*

God sat Sunday in her Adirondack deck chair
reading the New York Times and sipping strawberry lemonade
her pink robe flowing down to the ground

the garment hem was fluff and frill
and it spilled holiness down into the sanctuary
into the cup and the nostrils of the singing people

one thread trickled loveliness into a funeral rite
as the mourners looked in the face of death
and heard the story of a life truer than goodness

a torn piece of the robe's edge flopped onto
a war in southern Sudan and caused heartbeats
to skip and soldiers looked into themselves deeply

one threadbare strand of the divine belt
almost knocked over a polar bear floating
on a loose berg in the warming sea

one silky string wove its way through Jesus' cross
and tied itself to desert-parched immigrants with swollen tongues
and a woman with ovarian cancer and two young sons

you won't believe this, but a single hair-thin fiber
floated onto the yacht of a rich man and he gasped
when he saw everything as it really was

the hem fell to and fro across the universe
filling space and time and gaps between the sub-atomic world
with the effervescent presence of the one who is the is

and even in the slight space between lovers in bed
the holiness flows and wakes up the body
to feel beyond the feeling and know beyond the knowing

and even as we monotheize and trinitize
and speculate and doubt even our doubting
the threads of holiness trickle into our lives

and the seraphim keep singing "holy, holy, holy"
and flapping their wings like baby birds
and God says: give it a rest a while

and God takes another sip of her summertime drink
and smiles at the way you are reading this filament now
and hums: It's a good day to be God

# Institutionalized Jesus

*Lectionary 10 B*
Mark 3:20–35

*When his family heard it, they went out to restrain him, for people were saying, "He has gone out of his mind." (Mark 3:21)*

he is out of his mind, can't you see?
you get the straight jacket and
I'll get the hypodermic sedative
maybe we can restrain and institutionalize him enough
so his insidious words and soul-rending power
will stop harassing us to the threshold
of transformation and the terrifying life
of living in utter abandon in the universal love

he is out of his mind, isn't he?
he is too far gone to be domesticated
like a grazing bovine chewing its cud
like us eating and spitting up
and chewing and swallowing obsessive-compulsively
the same old fibrous indigestible news
that this life is only what we earn and spend
protect and steal, war over and control

he is out of his mind, right?
his gyrating irises look so full of larger consciousness
his nostrils flare with majestic being and potency and spirit
maybe if we loosen one or two straps
on his gurney, maybe if we let him writhe and speak

a couple more words of astonishing goodness
he can crack our skulls and let loose our suffering brains
our restraints, our imprisoning anodyne normalcies
and we might live in his craziness
meld with his love, his enthusiastic holistic mind
not he out of his, but we out of ours

# Automatic Earth

*Lectionary 11 B*
Mark 4:26–34

*He also said, "The kingdom of God is as if someone would scatter seed on
the ground, and would sleep and rise night and day, and the seed would
sprout and grow, he does not know how. (Mark 4:26–27)*

The automatic earth does her spinning thing while you
nap and eat buttered toast and make love,
walk the dog, curse at the traffic, make plans for next Tuesday
and forget why you went upstairs with the hammer

the wheat head bursts forth and spills seed
into the soil, interred and forgotten—
just like you fear your burial, your englobement
—but remembered by the sun-warmed humus and the sun's sun

the river does not need you to push it with paddle or oar
the flower does not require you to pry its petals open
the clouds glide effortlessly without you puckering and blowing
the sea tides obey lunar expertise and not yours

yet you thinking you must do something
with your MBA skills and calculus and voting ballot
you thinking that you must do something
for the magic to happen

all the while the divine mystery seducing you
to breathe slowly in and out,
to release the urge to cause or be caused
to do nothing and be the universe entire

# What Job Meant to Say Had He Girded Up His Loins

*Lectionary 12 B*
Job 38:1–11

> *Then the LORD answered Job out of the whirlwind: "Who is this that darkens counsel by words without knowledge? Gird up your loins like a man, I will question you, and you shall declare to me. (Job 38:1–3)*

Since you queried, O Great One, where I was
while you were expanding space
slamming atoms together, kneading time to sticky dough,
doing that song and dance with planets, coaxing corpuscles,

I was weaving reeds together into rope
and using rope to scale the mountain
standing atop the mountain on tippy toes
reaching up to the stars you playfully put beyond my reach

and then looking out at the sea and the waves
you contain with gates and walls of land
I saw the dolphins pirouette and sea spray fly
and I picked up a praying mantis and we prayed as one

what else could we crickets of men and women do but answer
your rhetorical questions with such gorgeous, harmonized chirps

# The Bread that Satisfies

*Lectionary 17 B*
John 6:1–21

*Then Jesus took the loaves, and when he had given thanks, he distributed*
*them to those who were seated; so also the fish, as much as they wanted.*
*When they were satisfied, he told his disciples, "Gather up the fragments*
*left over, so that nothing may be lost." (John 6:11–12)*

Hungry, we cry for bread, but more than
barley or wheat or artisanal loaves,
beyond the chewing and swallowing and
stomach satisfaction it is the breaking
the placing in the hand the community rising
from shared sustenance like the magic of
yeast in the dough filling us up
satiating body, mind, and spirit
making us one with earth, brother, sister,
self, and you, holy companion,
the giver of all to all for all in all.

# Sense of Wisdom

*Lectionary 20 B*
Proverbs 9:1–6

> *Come, eat of my bread and drink of the wine I have mixed. Lay aside immaturity, and live, and walk in the way of insight. (Prov 9:5–6)*

wisdom knows that it does not know
so it knows it knows something

but that something is a speck of nothing
and in that speck of a nothing

is the beginning of knowing a something;
wisdom knows that the subject and object

and preposition and verb and participle
of all that can be known is the one divine

and so the only sentence uttered
that ever made any sense is

when a sole man, a lone woman,
looked up at the spattered starry sky

and looked in at the blood-pulsing heart
and felt the space between them collapse

in that immeasurably small grain of time
and he and she said:

God is here and not here
and now I know

# If Only We Had Better Options

*Lectionary 21 B*
John 6:56–69

> *So Jesus asked the twelve, "Do you also wish to go away?" Simon Peter answered him, "Lord, to whom can we go? You have the words of eternal life. We have come to believe and know that you are the Holy One of God." (John 6:67–69)*

do you also wish to go away
he asked and stunned us like electricity
and we whispered under our breath

yes we would like an easier path
clear cut through the oak forest
something that made sense at least

or better, we wish you would go away
Jesus, you keep complicating and confusing us
and messing us up so we can't think straight

if only we could have not known you
and heard your words that burn in us now
and never felt your spirit radiate its way through us

right on into the infinite *yes*
but then again, before you
was only the deafening finite *no*

and the deathtrap of our anxious breathless days
so, no, we don't want to go away
because, honestly, where would we go?

# Jesus: Cardiologist

*Lectionary 22 B*
Mark 7:1–8, 14–15, 21–23

> *For it is from within, from the human heart, that evil intentions come: fornication, theft, murder, adultery, avarice, wickedness, deceit, licentiousness, envy, slander, pride, folly. All these evil things come from within, and they defile a person." (Mark 7:21–23)*

you are all about heart work
a cardiologist of the soul

and so much less about gut work you say
it's not the outside coming in

and the digestion and the excrement
it's the inner life, the heart's desires

the mind's formation, the mouth's utterances
that you came to expose and name

and reshape into something life-giving
not life-diminishing which seems to be our way

before we suffer an arrest and infarct
you have come to scrape out our arteries

infuse us with your Lipitor grace
clarify us with your angioplastic mercy

prop us open with your stents of truth telling
letting the warmth of blood flow freely again

so every lub dub beating of our new hearts
can oxygenate our own active mercy

and shape our vocal chords for words of loving-kindness
and fill every corpuscle with hope

that the rhythmic drumming of our lives can sync
and syncopate with the cosmic cardiac pulse of God

# Lose Yourself Along the Way

*Lectionary 24 B*
Mark 8:27–38

*For those who want to save their life will lose it, and those who lose their*
*life for my sake, and for the sake of the gospel, will save it. (Mark 8:35)*


this road you pave with your words
and your broken body and blood poured

it is not on the lustrous map I bought on Amazon
the Travel Channel has no feature on the highlights and hot spots

there is no restaurant tour with stops for every palate
no kitschy giant dinosaurs to stop and take snapshots with the kids

this way that you speak of with mouth wide open
is every dark dream we ever feared might be true

and all that we wish we could fix about our lot
and the sum of all we reject and hide in the mind's black box

hoping we will never lose control and crash into the jungle
and have its contents played for all to hear

but you say this bumpy path, this crooked cross highway
is the way of life itself, the gift hidden inside ugly truth

that we will indeed know suffering no matter our resistance
but oh, letting it befriend us we finally have something to live for

something bigger than ourselves, so trembling we submit
and enter into your eddy of mercy and welcome the news

we live only when we have something we are willing to die for
when we know that our lives in their short span were spent for love

# Jesus and the Boys

*Lectionary 25 B*
Mark 9:30–37

*Then they came to Capernaum; and when he was in the house he asked
them, "What were you arguing about on the way?" But they were silent,
for on the way they had argued with one another who was the greatest.
He sat down, called the twelve, and said to them, "Whoever wants to be
first must be last of all and servant of all." (Mark 9:33–35)*

Like seven-year-olds wearing black capes
and flying through the green back yard

we spit and sputter in staccato speech
I'm the greatest . . . no I am . . . no really it's me

all while listening to our Jesus buddy ramble on
about betrayal and death and a whisper about after that

but we raise our pecan stick swords way high over head
and battle and pretend a beheaded victory

still the Nazareth dude nullifies our superhero powers
reminding us of the one thing that deflates grandiosity:

someone has come to serve you and lift you up
even you who imagines you alone lift yourself up

and so we crack the sticks on our knees, untie our capes
and pray: help us redefine greatness through you

help the boys let go of grasping after fake powers
help the boys become men with life to give away

# About that Plucking Out the Eye Thing

*Lectionary 26 B*
Mark 9:38–50

> *And if your eye causes you to stumble, tear it out; it is better for you to enter the kingdom of God with one eye than to have two eyes and to be thrown into hell, where their worm never dies, and the fire is never quenched. (Mark 9:47–48)*

One of them came in wet with a millstone and a rope
knotted around his throat gasping for air having dragged
the damn thing up from the bottom of the river
because he had cursed at a child for high-pitched screaming

Another came in with her right hand
hacked off—she was left-handed—
and she dripped crimson drops all the way
down the hall to Jesus' living room
admitting she had used the missing appendage
to flip someone off in traffic for cutting in

One more limped in with a lopped-off foot
in his hand and he dropped to the floor sobbing
because he had tripped someone in line
in front of him to get a better spot
at Bonnaroo this year to see Radiohead

Then there was the disciple who had an eye patch
and fumbled her way through the door
having glared at her next door neighbor with
a bitchy stare because she looked so freaking good
in that new dress and those shoes with red soles
and wished she would trip and tear her ACL

They gathered around Jesus, each face
with a seriousness that puzzled the good Lord
except for the one with the plucked out eye,
it was hard to look puzzled with the patch and all.
He looked at them and said trying not to laugh:

For God's sake, stop damaging yourselves.
You know I was kidding, right?
Have you heard of hyperbole?
Come on, folks! Get over yourselves!
You're not that bad, and you're not that good.

And then they ate supper and he taught them
many more things that they misunderstood.

# And He Took Them Up in His Arms

*Lectionary 27 B*
Mark 10:2–16

> *People were bringing little children to him in order that he might touch them; and the disciples spoke sternly to them. But when Jesus saw this, he was indignant and said to them, "Let the little children come to me; do not stop them; for it is to such as these that the kingdom of God belongs. Truly I tell you, whoever does not receive the kingdom of God as a little child will never enter it." And he took them up in his arms, laid his hands on them, and blessed them. (Mark 10:13–16)*

Make us enjoy bubbles blown in the wind
and chased after in giggling glee
before they pop and splatter on our faces

Move us to climb the summer night to the rooftop
watching the Perseid meteor shower till dawn's twilight
with guttural wows and oohs at the sparkling sky streaks

Give us energy for playing in the debris of the world
turning mud into castles and sticks into houses
and we imagine we are kings and queens again

Give us eyes to see an enchanted universe
where every magical dream and foolish hope
are possible and expected and make us giddy with anticipation

Take our sticky adult minds and thin our thick thoughts
until our flowing childhood wonder returns at every cricket
and we are moved by every chocolate kiss and lip kisses, too

until finally you elicit our antediluvian praise
and we sit back in your loving arms
and know very little except that we are and we are in you

# Calling All Jerks

*Lectionary 28 B*
Mark 10:17–31

> *Jesus, looking at him, loved him and said, "You lack one thing; go,*
> *sell what you own, and give the money to the poor, and you will have*
> *treasure in heaven; then come, follow me." When he heard this, he was*
> *shocked and went away grieving, for he had many possessions.*
> *(Mark 10:21–22)*

Like Steve Martin's Jerk
we think we only need
this one precious thing

a paddle game is all
and we will be satisfied
slogging out the door

until we see the TV remote
and pick it up with an artifice of glee
and mumble: this is all I need

but you know how this goes,
don't you fellow jerk?
one more thing will do it

and we will finally in our bones
against all past comic failures
be satisfied and done with grabbing

and then our de-jerkifying Jesus
stops us and tells us to let go
drop the lamp and put down the ashtray

let go of it all, including yourself, so we can grasp
the one thing we jerks are always questing for
and no, it is not a thermos

# Do for Us Whatever We Ask

*Lectionary 29 B*
Mark 10:35–45

> *James and John, the sons of Zebedee, came forward to him and said to him, "Teacher, we want you to do for us whatever we ask of you." And he said to them, "What is it you want me to do for you?" And they said to him, "Grant us to sit, one at your right hand and one at your left, in your glory." (Mark 10:35-37)*

Give us flimsy blue ribbons for first and second place
and a shiny plastic trophy for the dresser top
affirming our fragile, boyish, hurting egos

Make us more special than everyone else's specialness
put a sash around us and notice that adorable hair curl looping down
so you can truss up our needy, hungry girlish souls

Grant us every wish from Maseratis to mansions
and manufactured beauty to immaculate perfection
so all will be well and no grey spills through the cracks

Then watch us fall into predictable chemical dependency
as we crawl through the numb dumbness
of our lives made false and empty without scar or scuffle

Cry for us as we grieve the years gone by
and every chance we had to sacrifice our golden selves
was stopped by our boundless need to step on and over and win

Comfort us when we slip and somersault on the icy road
toward preciousness and piety and strawberry preserve sweetness
that keep us from ever feeling warm fleshly earthy life

as you did, as you loved with abandon every one and every thing
as you counted the cost of being vulnerably human and then
spent it all in every daily cross of getting yourself out of the way

and letting each Spirit-filled encounter with life's dirt and dander
urge and move you to crazy ways of embracing the pained
with the same holy hug that held you tight even through death

# Art of Reformation

*Reformation Sunday*
Jeremiah 31:31–34

> *But this is the covenant that I will make with the house of Israel after those days, says the LORD: I will put my law within them, and I will write it on their hearts; and I will be their God, and they shall be my people. (Jer 31:33)*

You can take a hunk of brown moist modeling clay
squeeze it in your hands and eye it oozing between fingers
like ribbons rolling out on the table top

shape it into a dove or a fish or a water bowl
maybe throw it on the wheel and tactilely
coax it into a vase or an abstraction of yourself

and then having reshaped the stoic block into sculpture
you have to decide: put it in the kiln and fire it
preserve its beauty in brittle perfection

or keep it supple and soft, wet and moving
so that when the times require creative reformation
you can give thanks for the dove, the bowl, the vase

then reimagine what this poetic mud can be
and spin a chalice or hand-shape a plate
and invite everyone to bring the bread and wine

or get a camera and pose the earthy medium
flip the shutter once, repose, shoot again
and make this reformation into claymation

animation of the potter Spirit keeping all things fluid
aquifying calcified statues like you and me and church
freeing our joints to be the art of God's desire

# Lazarus Acrostic

*All Saints / All Souls*
John 11:32–44

> *When he had said this, he cried with a loud voice, "Lazarus, come out!"*
> *The dead man came out, his hands and feet bound with strips of cloth, and*
> *his face wrapped in a cloth. Jesus said to them, "Unbind him, and*
> *let him go." (John 11:43-44)*

Lost to the earth four days, the rotting stench, suddenly the dead man
Aroused by holy, invigorating Spirit, but no B-movie
Zombie walking the earth for unspeakable hunger,
Against the pull of entropy, a sea voyage from hope, against all
Reason and wild expectations, this one shows the glory
Under the compulsion of compassion and love
See grief tears dripping from Jesus' face become a baptism from death to life

# The Widow and the Cross

*Lectionary 32 B*
Mark 12:38–44

*A poor widow came and put in two small copper coins, which are worth
a penny. Then he called his disciples and said to them, "Truly I tell you,
this poor widow has put in more than all those who are contributing to
the treasury. For all of them have contributed out of their abundance; but
she out of her poverty has put in everything she had, all she had to
live on." (Mark 12:42–44)*

Not a black spider with red hourglass on her back
Not a hairline peak on a combed-back forehead
Not a walk on the rooftop in wartime waiting

She, a woman intimate with grief's grip on her throat
She, a woman befriending fear like the neighbor's cat
She, a woman weak like candle smoke in men's windy ways

Jesus points his unmanicured finger her way, not theirs
Jesus extrapolates her silent penny to God, not their flapping bills and lips
Jesus notices her aloud, the mimetic gift of his own complete giving

Not an Easter bun with sweet drizzled icing
Not a verb for getting to the other side of the street
Not an ornament for church or neck or ring

# Rumors

*Lectionary 33 B*
Mark 13:1–8

> *When you hear of wars and rumors of wars, do not be alarmed; this*
> *must take place, but the end is still to come. For nation will rise against*
> *nation, and kingdom against kingdom; there will be earthquakes in vari-*
> *ous places; there will be famines. This is but the beginning of the*
> *birth pangs. (Mark 13:7–8)*

Did you hear the murmurs that things are going black
and lockstep war is coming that will horrify and crush
and there's nothing you or the generals can do about it?

Did the gossip train roar by your way today
and Doppler shift whistle that stars are disintegrating
and temples and towers falling while we watch with small eyes?

Did the word mushroom to your state that a virus leaked
and the military lost control of containment
and soon North Dakota will be silent and then South?

Listen: It's all true, or it's freaked out fearful chatter, or who knows,
but then what anyway? All is prologue and prelude, lift up your
heart to the universe, the ultimate word and song are yet to come:

sonnets of peace, grace notes of loving-kindness, rumors spreading
of Spirit filling up the desolate space between when all this
cosmic crucifixion will rest and then rise a sanctified singularity

# Calling All Kings

*Christ the King Sunday*
John 18:33–37

> *Pilate asked him, "So you are a king?" Jesus answered, "You say that I am a king. For this I was born, and for this I came into the world, to testify to the truth. Everyone who belongs to the truth listens to my voice." (John 18:37)*

Let those men who know and trust their inner king
who trust their own power
and don't misuse it,
who live beyond themselves
who see the greater vision
who seek blessing for all
who create order out of chaos
who foster peace in themselves and others—
let them embody their king today,
humbly yet boldly,
fearlessly and with joyful strength,
for this world is short on men
who know they have generative power to give life away
and so many turn to false kings
boys who think a crown costume is all they need
who stomp and plunder and turn the land to ruin
who sound the war siren
without counting the cost
and forget that caring for the weakest among us
and uniting the land as one
are the reason there are kings at all.

# Lectionary Year C

# You Said Meet You by the Fig Tree

*Advent 1 C*
Luke 21:25–36

> *Then he told them a parable: "Look at the fig tree and all the trees; as soon as they sprout leaves you can see for yourselves and know that summer is already near. So also, when you see these things taking place, you know that the kingdom of God is near. (Luke 21:29–31)*

You said meet you by the fig tree
and the leaves would heal us
and the branches flower and fruit and feed

you said God would appear as sure as spring
and something wonderful that has no human words,
maybe only exhalations, was coming, and soon, and how

we waited by the tree, observed fruit emerging,
heard it plunk to the ground, smelled sweet softened flesh
watched chipmunks and marmosets scurry off with it all

now the leaves brown and pirouette to the ground
and the branches look like weapons and the wind blows
through us and we are naked in our waiting in our weakened faith

you admonish, "Be on guard, let not your hearts be weighed down
with dissipation and drunkenness and worry," but
gravity pulls and tugs and we do droop and drink and dissolve

O Lord, yes you—the one who said to meet you there
the one who withered on the tree like wasted produce
who rose too soon because where are you now—our longing for you aches

so why do we gather still and so, watching twigs sprout and bud
spying every last *ficus carica*, eavesdropping to hear if you will curse it
or finally flower all hopes and dreams now shriveled on the branch

# The Messenger

*Advent 2 C*
Malachi 3:1–4

*See, I am sending my messenger to prepare the way before me, and the
LORD whom you seek will suddenly come to his temple. The messenger
of the covenant in whom you delight—indeed, he is coming, says the
LORD of hosts. But who can endure the day of his coming, and who
can stand when he appears? For he is like a refiner's fire and like fullers'
soap; he will sit as a refiner and purifier of silver, and he will purify the
descendants of Levi and refine them like gold and silver, until they present offerings to the LORD in righteousness. (Mal 3:1–3)*

comes in midnight dreams to tell us that the mountain of ore—
five tons of debris from the soul's strip mine
dug up from psychotherapy and silent desert sitting
exposing veins of pain and subterranean turpitude—
looks like a waste of dirt and igneous rock and tailings
but is all there for the intended divine distillation
the pyre of grace and the crucible of mercy
until sitting in the bottom of the vaporized pile
is the gold of your true self too long entombed
and now, even in your resistance to purification,
shines like the harvest moon low over the city
slowly rising to the apex of holy night happenings

# Gaudete

*Advent 3 C*
Philippians 4:4–7

*Rejoice in the Lord always; again I will say, Rejoice. (Phil 4:4)*

Gaudete you say
Gaudete in Domino semper
and the steering wheel slips to the right
and the car crash comes quickly
and the concussion disorients without disabling

Gaudete you say
Gaudete in Domino semper
and the scud missiles fly wildly
and the neighbor's daughter is damaged
and rifle fire never ceases in the night

Gaudete you say
Gaudete in Domino semper
and eyes scan the cityscape for connections
and the forlorn touch only touch screens
and the suicidal pray through pain for relief

Gaudete you say
and what else can we do
but rejoice always in you
the rejoicing a defiance and
balm and peace and communion

# Magnifying Glass

*Advent 4 C*
Luke 1:39–55

*And Mary said, "My soul magnifies the Lord, (Luke 1:46)*

We hear that down is up and up is down
rich empty and poor, poverty steeped with riches
and nothing will ever be the same

Our pride is exposed as shame and
shame inverted becomes pride
and nothing will ever be the same

The kings beg in the street for coins and
the street junkies take eucalyptus steam showers all day
and nothing will ever be the same

You come into this gunning, shot-up world
Mary sings of your power and peace
and your only weapon a willing womb

You magnify us with your round looking glass
and see our microscopic lives as large
and our greatness you smoke out with focused light

In turn our souls magnify you, you unexpected world flipper,
as we look up through the lens of goodness and mercy
and just your eye fills up the monocle of the sky

# Epiphany One Way or Another

*Epiphany*
Matthew 2:1–12

> *When they had heard the king, they set out; and there, ahead of them,*
> *went the star that they had seen at its rising, until it stopped over the*
> *place where the child was. When they saw that the star had stopped, they*
> *were overwhelmed with joy. (Matt 2:9–10)*

For you it might be a magic light
appearing in the beckoning western sky
you follow it despite the peril and ridiculous cosmology
find what you were looking for in a backwater town
and rejoice in your bones that for a moment
you were breathless with holy hope
and then when a dream tells you to turn left at Jerusalem
you turn left and never look back or reappear or question
but still, you found it, you felt it, you lucky star-gazing fool

For me it was a slow mystery emerging from darkness
a sliver of silver working its way through
the hairline cracks of my life:
my father's young death and the family shuffling
the unfulfilled longings of home and stable ground
my mother's short cobbled path and leaving me a 28-year-old orphan
the broken promises I can never unbreak
my sons' beautiful and unbearable limited reality
the day I found our cat dead and bloated under the deck

the midlife falling into bottomless blackness
and the unforeseen and unknown father's strong catch
and then, emerging like Venus through January clouds,
the Epiphany, the star, the shining that only comes in the night

# On Taking the Watery Plunge

**Baptism of Our Lord**
Luke 3:15–17, 21–22

*Now when all the people were baptized, and when Jesus also had been baptized and was praying, the heaven was opened, and the Holy Spirit descended upon him in bodily form like a dove. And a voice came from heaven, "You are my Son, the Beloved; with you I am well pleased."*
*(Luke 3:21–22)*

you could dig yourself a smooth-edged open grave
or find the garden for your eventual scattering
and place a chiseled stone or etched plaque there
with your name and birth date and a dash
then you could visit this truth-space when your ego's adrift or
every day even and touch your dimensional name
maybe make a rubbing with black crayon and charcoal paper
say hello to your once and future self
being gentle with what was which is still yet to be
and giving thanks for what is and has now slipped away
or you could find a pool,
a river, an ocean
and plunge
yourself in,
or rather
be plunged
by mystery's invitation
and drown to yourself today and breath under water this future
living now into tomorrow what already was not yet

free from your intestinal fear at the very first shovel of dirt
and contemplation of your underground sepulcher
or the sight of the flower in the garden
that grows blue from the minerals in your bones

# Today

*Lectionary 3 C*
Luke 4:14–21

> *Then he began to say to them, "Today this scripture has been fulfilled in your hearing." (Luke 4:21)*

Yes, you can look back at all the clouded midnights
and the miserable poor who overflow
the urban cups of containment
and the blind and lame and deaf who
bump and toddle along next to all the
eyes and legs and ears never scarred
and sob for past imprisonments that cannot be redeemed

Yes, you can look ahead to the dreamy day
when all is well and all shall be well
and the present day hipster cynic
will be crushed by joy and released from dire irony
and then sit there and grieve the time gorge
between then and this sorry now
and fall into the groove of post-everything sarcasm

Or, you can look into now and see the glory
hidden in the cracks and fissures of reality
a paucity of light, yes, but still seeping through
glory in the poor who manufacture joy from nothing
glory in the blind who make their way just fine thank you
glory in the deaf who make tacit words you wish you could hear

glory in the locked up who discover inner sovereignty
glory in the one word spoken you've never wagered on
today is the day and liberation is now
and not even your ferocious doubt
or lingering melancholia can disable it
but your surrender to its unmitigated truth
collapses all of time into this eternal munificent is

# Oh Boy Jeremiah

*Lectionary 4 C*
Jeremiah 1:4–10

*Then I said, "Ah, Lord GOD! Truly I do not know how to speak, for I am only a boy." But the LORD said to me, "Do not say, 'I am only a boy'; for you shall go to all to whom I send you, and you shall speak whatever I command you. Do not be afraid of them, for I am with you to deliver you. (Jer 1:6–8)*

He heard a voice that only men hear when ears open
put down his blue light saber removed his holster and belt

disassembled his Lego kingdom castle
and retired his knights and horses and trebuchet

boxed up the green Army men with frozen pea faces
and decommissioned the generals and their monochrome medals

put his red-tipped pistol in the garbage with the Mountain Dew
and tossed the paper-tape caps and plasticized badge

the boy heeded his interior for the first time and convulsed
at the call to be strong in word and muscle and heart and will

the yearning to do holy things for magnanimous purposes
and drop pretense and armor and put his own flesh on

he looked at his father's leathered hands
his uncle's gray hair and grandfather's worn out body

he weighed the heft of work ahead against the helium frivolity
of youth and so he said to the Spirit that haunted him

oh boy, he said, it looks too hard for this boy
and the Spirit said to the one naked without toys, oh man

# Hidden in Plain Sight

*Transfiguration C*
Luke 9:28–43

*Now about eight days after these sayings Jesus took with him Peter and John and James, and went up on the mountain to pray. And while he was praying, the appearance of his face changed, and his clothes became dazzling white. (Luke 9:28–29)*

You the Easter egg
gingerly hidden in plain sight as playful revelation
once glowing on crisp air mountaintop
now seen in dank gory warfare trenches
bloody hands laboring for immigrant dinners
stupefied whiskey winners standing on desperate penthouse ledges
yearning to be revealed in every moment's existential dread
will anyone look behind the wispy curtain in every room and field
and see your lighted bittersweet face,
sentinel as a distant lighthouse
to the unbounded love
in each bounded, woeful, brilliant life

# Ash Thursday

*Ash Wednesday*
Joel 2:1–2, 12–17

> *Blow the trumpet in Zion; sanctify a fast; call a solemn assembly.*
> *(Joel 2:15)*

He did the yearly black solemn ritual
and got smeared and humbled though he
didn't like it much with the flecks falling down
in his eyelashes and the soul's grief exposed so

He got home and stared at his conundrummed face
for five minutes give or take in the bathroom mirror
it wrecked him to be so humiliated, so mortified
he washed away the ashen cross and dreamed of dying

He woke up Thursday and after peeing and scratching
looked in the mirror and there it was like a Mardi Gras drunken tattoo
his forehead graffitied, black, sooty,
haunting him he wore it all day like an unbandaged wound

At bedtime that night he washed and slept like a storm-tossed boat
woke up to his sunrise reflection, his sleet eyes squinted
again it was back, his skin tagged with midnight streaks
and he walked the day mortal through to his marrow

After that first Ash Thursday and Ash Friday
and Ash Tomorrow, Ash Next Week
Ash March, Ash Autumn, Ash Solstices
never a day went by when he didn't see it, let it have its way

Never a day went by thereafter that he didn't
rise to bless himself with Wednesdays words:
remember you are dust and to dust you shall return
and every day then on he was his free earthy self until he died

# The Wanderer

*Lent 1 C*
Deuteronomy 26:1–11

> *You shall make this response before the LORD your God: "A wandering Aramean was my ancestor; he went down into Egypt and lived there as an alien, few in number, and there he became a great nation, mighty and populous." (Deut 26:5)*

From Aramea to Los Angeles to San Antonio
he wandered until something said get landed

he bought a condo once in Manhattan at 84th
but locked the door one day and walked away for good

settled down in Indiana for a spell on the prairie
but got the itch to hitchhike down the wildflower highway

got married and had his sons and thought
that meant they all had to be rooted like old vines

read one day that his grandfather never owned land
and they told legends about his messy masculine life

heard his father say that his worst year of life
was 1954 when he mortgaged his unfettered joy

chanted in liturgy on Sunday that all his faith ancestors
were wanderers the likes of Abraham and Sarah

walked the via crucis in one holy week and found
his feet less stuck to the clay earth below

# Deep and Terrifying Darkness in which Covenant Comes

*Lent 2 C*
Genesis 15:1–12, 17–18

> *As the sun was going down, a deep sleep fell upon Abram, and a deep*
> *and terrifying darkness descended upon him. When the sun had gone*
> *down and it was dark, a smoking fire pot and a flaming torch passed be-*
> *tween these pieces. On that day the LORD made a covenant with Abram,*
> *saying, "To your descendants I give this land, from the river of Egypt to*
> *the great river, the river Euphrates. (Gen 15:12, 17–18)*

It's the moment when you see all the stars
in one eye's retina and you count up
from Betelgeuse to googolplex
and fall into the universe swallowed whole

It's the time when you hiked the Grand Canyon
on the Hermit Trail and your foot slipped off
the thin concave path high above the unforgiving river and
you grabbed a sapling's single branch placed just in reach

It's the dream when you envisioned the smoking fire pot
and the flaming torch promenading through
the slain and split heifer, goat, and ram and see
you are still whole and blessed and counted among the stars

It's the eternal now in which you still your twitchy mind
and in the stillness a tremulous quiet and in the quiet
a numinous nothing and in the nothing the one who creates
out of it celestial and terrestrial wonderment like Sirius and you

# Yours Not Mine
# (Unless with Yours)

*Lent 3 C*
Isaiah 55:1–9

*For my thoughts are not your thoughts, nor are your ways my ways, says*
*the LORD. For as the heavens are higher than the earth, so are my ways*
*higher than your ways and my thoughts than your thoughts. (Isa 55:8–9)*

My thoughts get tangled in neurons, lost at dopamined synapses
frenzied as they striate my cerebrum and trip through my dreams

Your thoughts penetrate midnight in sublime linear streaks
and turn nighttime into stippled light and placid shade

My ways are a crapshoot with loaded dice mismatched
so two always rolls with two and I go bust and martini drunk

Your ways are counterpoint and harmony that lull and then stun
with intervals and variations turning notes into soulful healing

Your thoughts are not my thoughts so the world is thought clear
mindfulness fills the cosmos and even my own skull-trapped mind

Your ways are not my ways so there may be a way yet to wade my way
through this river of crosses and freestyle to Ezekiel's tree-lined shore

# When the Manna Ran Out

*Lent 4 C*
Joshua 5:9–12

*The manna ceased on the day they ate the produce of the land, and the Israelites no longer had manna; they ate the crops of the land of Canaan that year. (Josh 5:12)*

We got so used to plucking manna flakes off the ground
feeding on evening quail rotisseried over campfire
filling calf stomach casks with cleft-rock water

we thought this was the gift and the divine life
to wake every morning with nothing to do save
sweep up breakfast and grab dinner by the squawking throat

but when the manna gave out and the quail and the flowing rock
our fingers rubbed raw from plucking low grain and high fruit
and our backs ached from hauling water from the far creek

another grace appeared, a new holy bequest exceeding the first
our tired frames gathered for dinner round the embers
and we ate and sang heaven-sent thanks for our bodies that work

# Spikenard

*Lent 5 C*
John 12:1–8

> *Mary took a pound of costly perfume made of pure nard, anointed
> Jesus' feet, and wiped them with her hair. The house was filled with the
> fragrance of the perfume. But Judas Iscariot, one of his disciples (the one
> who was about to betray him), said, Why was this perfume not sold for
> three hundred denarii and the money given to the poor? (John 12:3–5)*

*from Wikipedia:*

Spikenard (Nardostachys jatamansi)
also called nard, nardin, and muskroot
is a flowering plant of the Valerian family
that grows in the Himalayas of Nepal, China, and India.

The plant grows to about one meter in height
and has pink, bell-shaped flowers.
It is found in the altitude
of about 3000–5000 meters.

Spikenard rhizomes
can be crushed and distilled
into an intensely aromatic
amber-colored essential oil,
which is very thick in consistency.

Nard oil is used as a perfume,
an incense, a sedative,
and an herbal medicine said to fight
insomnia, birth difficulties,
and other minor ailments.

The scent of spikenard attracts cats,
a strange phenomenon in itself

*from the New Testament:*

An anointing oil used
to prepare Jesus' body
by a woman who perfumed him
with expense and honor

the cause of men's grousing
about waste and the poor
and turning the mind away
from the obvious costly
outpouring and crushing

medicine so their other ailments
might find healing
and they might be as cats to nard
attracted to an intensely aromatic God

a strange phenomenon in itself

# Palm or Passion, Wave or Particle

*Palm Sunday / Sunday of the Passion C*
Luke 22:14—23:56

> *Then Jesus, crying with a loud voice, said, "Father, into your hands I commend my spirit." Having said this, he breathed his last. When the centurion saw what had taken place, he praised God and said, "Certainly this man was innocent." (Luke 23:46-47)*

They say in quantum physics that a particle
is a wave and a wave a particle
and it all depends on how you look and when
but if you don't look for the answer,
if you let paradox be and mystery win
it is both at the same time all at once

Jesus and his little royal palm parade
with branches waving and people shouting
everyone focuses their eyes and minds
like electron microscopes to see it
but looking there and then means
you only see the particle of fabricated greatness
but look another way and see the wave of humility
the rippling fall from the temporal throne,
the tsunami cross, the end that begins everything

I suppose the trick is not to look at all
but let it be and he will both ride to glory
and die in abject misery,
and one will be the other all at the same time
the cat will be dead and alive in the dark box
and you'll have to live in this puzzlement
and be both dead and alive yourself

# Mimetic Jesus

*Maundy Thursday*
John 13:1–17, 31b–35

*I give you a new commandment, that you love one another. Just as I have
loved you, you also should love one another. By this everyone will know
that you are my disciples, if you have love for one another.*
*(John 13:34-35)*

Let me not only imitate you
O foot washing Lord
who genuflects before me
O faithful friend
to the end and the end after that
O brother in flesh and spirit
who will not abandon me

Let me also desire what you desire
give me the heart that is your heart
let me love what you love

the servant mind and hand and muscle
who washes another's worn out sole
the faithful companion
who walks beyond the end of the clear-cut path
the brother in arms
of brother or sister or stranger
who will not let go
will not let go

# Living Jesus

*Resurrection of Our Lord C*
Luke 24:1–12

> *But on the first day of the week, at early dawn, they came to the tomb,*
> *taking the spices that they had prepared. They found the stone rolled*
> *away from the tomb, but when they went in, they did not find the*
> *body. (Luke 24:1–3)*

O Dead Jesus,
we remember the one day we had
two at best, to walk away in sadness
yes, but also in unshackled freedom,
free from your hard way,
free to live for ourselves only
free to walk utterly alone and in illusory control
making our way down the freeway
driving ourselves and each other crazy
crumpling and bursting into flames in the guardrail
but at least we weren't following your road
the way of crosses and costly love
and bodies spent

O Living Jesus
you are the next day of this crashed life
when we can no longer live
our lazy daydream life in and of and for ourselves
now we who follow you our brother and friend,
eating broken-body-bread and bloodshed-wine
living in the ethereal Spirit of your haunting presence

now we find ourselves unexpectedly
mysteriously, resistantly, and joyfully
living Jesus as our new selves-in-action
out of control in loving and giving and praising
and out of our minds in following you
where ever your next crazy offering
of yourself-in-us may be

# Order of St. Thomas

*Easter 2 C*
John 20:19–31

> *But Thomas (who was called the Twin), one of the twelve, was not with them when Jesus came. So the other disciples told him, "We have seen the Lord." But he said to them, "Unless I see the mark of the nails in his hands, and put my finger in the mark of the nails and my hand in his side, I will not believe." (John 20:24–25)*

If we could just believe and oh we would
if we could put our fingers in the nail marks
hands in the spear-gashed side

work our way into him up to our elbows
and then a shoulder and a foot
and climb into his woundedness completely

peer through his eyes and see what it's like
to walk this world resurrected and free
from death's power to box you up with ribbon

live in his accomplishments safe in his flesh
inoculated from any future punctures and bleeding
nuzzle up to his soothing heartbeat lullaby

But we won't get that, we won't even get belief
we have only to walk the way of vulnerable love
only to find him in every cut and broken bone

only to surrender as we keenly gaze
into our own open wounds and universal pain
only to find resurrection there inside us

And in our disbelief we will praise
in our mistrust we will worship
in our fear we will follow

# Oh, to Be as Bad as Paul

**Easter 3 C**
Acts 9:1–6

*Meanwhile Saul, still breathing threats and murder against the disciples*
*of the Lord, went to the high priest and asked him for letters to the*
*synagogues at Damascus, so that if he found any who belonged to the*
*Way, men or women, he might bring them bound to Jerusalem. Now as*
*he was going along and approaching Damascus, suddenly a light from*
*heaven flashed around him. (Acts 9:1–3)*

You waited for your Damascus blinding flash
and all you got was tourist cameras and smartphones
capturing a wisp of history at the roadside marker

You waited to get knocked off your electric horse
and all you got was a circling carnival pony ride
when you were five and all was wonder and wow

You waited for your own scaly-eyed vision of glory
and all you got was a long fall back to earth
and your highs were humbled like a poor man's dreams

You waited in the dark on the ground in dirt and dung
humility sucking you down deep like Tarzan's quicksand
and then in giving up you were called by name and rose up

# Suspense

*Easter 4 C*
John 10:22–30

*At that time the festival of the Dedication took place in Jerusalem. It was*
*winter, and Jesus was walking in the temple, in the portico of Solomon.*
*So the Jews gathered around him and said to him, "How long will you*
*keep us in suspense? If you are the Messiah, tell us plainly."*
*(John 10:22–23)*

That wonderful aching moment with crippled Jimmy Stewart
camera zooming through the rear window at Raymond Burr
the apartment door opening and the battle and the flash,
but then a quick resolve and denouement and credits and black

Hitchcock held us protracted in that anxious splendor in the
pause where it could go one way or the other and we wonder
longer than we expected or understood or even desired
but then not long enough once it ended and all was clear

How long will you keep us in suspense they asked
and Jesus knew better than Hitch or Kubrick not to answer clearly
but to hold them, suspend them, in the mystery of who
and what and when and how the divine would come through the door

and when it comes, would it knock down and overcome
would it accuse and accost and imprison
or would it shepherd and guide slowly, keeping us in suspense
for such long-held agonizing ecstasy as never to ask how long

# Glory Comes in Love

*Easter 5 C*
John 13:31–35

> *When he had gone out, Jesus said, "Now the Son of Man has been glori-*
> *fied, and God has been glorified in him. (John 13:31)*

He drove the majestic boulevard
his onyx black Mercedes shining
his thoughts wandered from board room
to stock rise and then to cabernets with legs

his mind queried and raced and fumbled
searching for something in him
that could ascend and hover above the ground
and find its way to the infinite light

until his car stopped at the crash the death
the injured child the woeful mother
and he stooped and dabbed blood and tears
took off his laundered shirt to bandage

and swaddled the whole mess in his soul
and sat and cried with those who cried
and wiped the boy's filthy, naked feet
and in a thin drip of light saw the glory

# Did You Dream Tonight

*Easter 6 C*
Revelation 21:10, 22—22:5

> *And in the spirit he carried me away to a great, high mountain and showed me the holy city Jerusalem coming down out of heaven from God. I saw no temple in the city, for its temple is the Lord God the Almighty and the Lamb. And the city has no need of sun or moon to shine on it, for the glory of God is its light, and its lamp is the Lamb.*
> *(Rev 21:10, 22–23)*

Did you dream tonight and
if you did was it good, was it holy
was it light and love in one colored vision
did the woven blanket wrap around you
like your spellbound embrace in electric REM cycle

or did you dream of earthquakes and bombs
heartache and disease and abandonment
a boy in the dry dirt thinner than straw
a girl alone on a honking city street island
a falling without flying that never ends

Did you feed your voracious mind
with blackness and gunshot and
the worst of yourself projected on screens
all the obvious waste of human living
like Tater Tots tossed in the mouth
without tasting beyond salt and fat
without nourishing any part of your hungry self

Or did you suckle on the milk of the soul
the new Jerusalem coming down a miasma
and lifting to unveil the community and canon song
and humble look in another's eye that says
we are in this together to stumble along
until we watch each other die and our grandchildren
bury us and remember us with gentle yearning
that we loved and we dreamed of love
and the reveries we had in the long nights of unknowing
were good and were always drawing us on
toward the dream of God into which we shall all awake

# Unity Complex

*Easter 7 C*
John 17:20–26

*I ask not only on behalf of these, but also on behalf of those who will be-*
*lieve in me through their word, that they may all be one. As you, Father,*
*are in me and I am in you, may they also be in us, so that the world may*
*believe that you have sent me. (John 17:20–21)*

One can be the singular one
or it can be arithmetically generous
a trillion divided by itself held as fraction

this unity you pray for is it
a lock-step compliance, an orthodoxy
the twentieth century hegemonic earthquake

is it school uniforms and khakis
blue polos and neckerchiefs tied just so
sneakers with white socks pulled up

or is it a complex of color differentiated
a polyrhythmic dance, a tango
of entanglement and then release

# God Stuck Her Tongue Out

*Pentecost*
Acts 2:1–21

*When the day of Pentecost had come, they were all together in one place.
And suddenly from heaven there came a sound like the rush of a violent
wind, and it filled the entire house where they were sitting. Divided
tongues, as of fire, appeared among them, and a tongue rested on each of
them. All of them were filled with the Holy Spirit and began to speak in
other languages, as the Spirit gave them ability. (Acts 2:1–4)*

God stuck her tongue out at the church
and we grabbed hold of the budded thing

and started flapping it around the neighborhood
like a swimming pool noodle or downy pillow

and before we knew it we were speaking things
we never bothered to dream or wonder

held our tight lips taut when we ever felt them
and yet there they were waggling out:

welcome, stranger, into the fold of mercy
now you are called brother, sister, friend

gather round, immigrants, we speak your language,
no one will shun your accent or poverty here

dance your way through the door, lost ones
and teach us your wild moves and we will teach ours

stroll in you wounded souls and skins
and let us wrap and kiss your pain to healing

make room, settled ones, for the wave is surging
and it will unsettle your closed-mouth silence

nothing, not even our provincial proclivities
can stop these mouths from sputtering

words of grace that blow open any door
any wall any blue law Sunday limitations

on what Spirit can do when set free to
tousle the world's hair

until love has swept us all away
and away and away beyond that

# Ease of Mystery

*Holy Trinity*
John 16:12–15

> *When the Spirit of truth comes, he will guide you into all the truth; for*
> *he will not speak on his own, but will speak whatever he hears, and he*
> *will declare to you the things that are to come. He will glorify me, be-*
> *cause he will take what is mine and declare it to you. All that the Father*
> *has is mine. For this reason I said that he will take what is mine and*
> *declare it to you. (John 16:13–15)*

not that it is hard as calculus or Rubik's Cube
but it is easier than thinking itself

not that you must own it or master it
but it contains you within itself generously

not that you can bottle it like spring water
but you walk through it like forest mist

not that you can keep it safe from adulteration
but you let it unlock you into the mess of life

not that you can doctrinize and ontologize it
but you sing its praises in harmony and unity

not that you can teach it like Cartesian philosophy
but you look at it together like the Chicago Chagall

not that it is work for you to do before or after faith
but you climb on it like playground monkey bars

not that it is hidden in a wartime cipher
but it is the peace of this tacit knowing

# Worthy

*Lectionary 9 C*
Luke 7:1–10

*When they came to Jesus, they appealed to him earnestly, saying, "He is worthy of having you do this for him, for he loves our people, and it is he who built our synagogue for us." And Jesus went with them, but when he was not far from the house, the centurion sent friends to say to him, "Lord, do not trouble yourself, for I am not worthy to have you come under my roof; (Luke 7:4–6)*

If someone said: dip a thin litmus strip into a beaker
full of a spinning alcohol distillation of you

would it satisfy a judging of your acerbic self
would it prove anything about the whether

and if of your life and your place in this spiral galaxy
and how close you are permitted to spin toward holiness

could someone send your DNA off to a sterile lab in Quantico
and decode your worth and potential and inevitable cause of death

maybe a hidden camera somewhere is scanning your retina
looking for some reason to let you in the door or rather not

instead, stand in the free wind and breathe in
and let the whirl of oxygen redden your blood

chant in ancient melody lines that you exist without apology
or regret, and you are foreign to nothing not even God

so offer your healing matchless praise with primitive abandon
while you still have breath and song and mind in space and time

# Oil and Wine

*Lectionary 15 C*
Luke 10:25–37

> *But a Samaritan while traveling came near him; and when he saw him,*
> *he was moved with pity. He went to him and bandaged his wounds, hav-*
> *ing poured oil and wine on them. Then he put him on his own animal,*
> *brought him to an inn, and took care of him. (Luke 10:33–34)*

Would you in the rush to capitalize on markets
in the anxiety of getting your life aligned just so

would you stop on the cracked roadside shoulder
where flat tire mishaps become robbery and assault

would you stop and nurse and neighbor me
tend the cuts and gashes to my body and mind

pour on the wine of compassion as antiseptic
smear the oil of mercy on me to bless and heal

or would you drive by and gape in the traffic slowdown
at the scene of a stranger in blood red calamity

let fear keep your own healing power stopped up
let our modern disconnection and despair keep your

oil and wine from ever touching another life
your hands from ever reaching out beyond your cuffs

never knowing you are the other I fear in my need
you the one who can heal us both

# Little Stranger Cakes

*Lectionary 16 C*
Genesis 18:1–10a

*Let me bring a little bread, that you may refresh yourselves, and after*
*that you may pass on — since you have come to your servant." So they*
*said, "Do as you have said." And Abraham hastened into the tent to*
*Sarah, and said, "Make ready quickly three measures of choice flour,*
*knead it, and make cakes." (Gen 18:5–6)*

When making little cakes for surprise visitors as your
obligatory hospitality, it is best not to kneed them too much
pat and coat them with some olive oil and if you have it
a dusting of crushed rosemary and fresh cracked pepper

then throw them in the beehive oven and let them brown
and crisp and rise slightly and then fall back like breathing
get your wooden paddle and slide it under to fetch them
put them on your pottery plate and serve hot with fresh salted cheese

as the three guests at your table take a bite and chew and smile
and you take the small one for yourself and listen to their wayfarer's tale
right then you'll know why numinous foreigners came your way tonight
why their words sound like holy mysteries plucked from behind the stars

when they leave you with their astonishing message and wander
down the ancient road to some other hopeless souls like you
who thought all that was left was decrepit aging and death, wash up
go to bed, give thanks for obligations, wild strange angels,
    and every coming birth

# Shuttered Doors and Detours

*Lectionary 17 C*
Luke 11:1–13

> *So I say to you, Ask, and it will be given you; search, and you will find;*
> *knock, and the door will be opened for you. For everyone who asks*
> *receives, and everyone who searches finds, and for everyone who knocks,*
> *the door will be opened. (Luke 11:9–10)*

When we return to poetry and myth and music
and put reason and intelligence in their proper place
which is to say a seat of limited honor and humbled praise
then we might be ready to listen to this Jesus strophe:

Knock, and the door will be opened.
Everyone who asks, receives.
Search, and you will find.
Persistence will be met with mercy.

But you stand there with your bloody rapping knuckles
and wonder what to do with shuttered doors and detours
because your tumor is growing apace with the calendar
your brimming pantry no longer satisfies anyone's nourishment

So you stop tapping and asking and searching
persistence gives way to the power of pain
like Abraham you give up the bargaining just short of total clemency
you think you have all the universe had to offer and you're done

But you'll always wonder, won't you, what absurd blessing would come
if you had knocked one more time with red bandages and waited
if you had kept questing beyond the rift of data with a run and a jump
and let holy imagination compose your future
with verse and metaphor, rhythm and melody

# Count the Stars

*Lectionary 19 C*
Genesis 15:1–6

> *He brought him outside and said, "Look toward heaven and count the stars, if you are able to count them." Then he said to him, "So shall your descendants be." And he believed the LORD; and the LORD reckoned it to him as righteousness. (Gen 15:5–6)*

Abraham's countless stars hover over our troubled heads
Sarah's skylights enlighten our skittish steps
our ancestors fill the night sky with testimony
this is not all there is, there is more to come
more than the terra and the ocean
the sky painter who flicks your future on midnight canvas
is making space for your story and song
making and guarding promises still unspoken
opening wormholes to times and places
unreachable by your linear, downward searching mind
so let that muscle in your forehead go and feel your brow drop
your heart slow and your brain relax and the flow flowing
and rocket on through fear until faith is your Milky Way

# Near and Far, I'm Afraid

*Lectionary 20 C*
Jeremiah 23:23–29

*Am I a God near by, says the LORD, and not a God far off? Who can
hide in secret places so that I cannot see them? says the LORD. Do I not
fill heaven and earth? says the LORD. (Jer 23:23–24)*


If I run to the Sangre de Cristo mountains
and disappear in New Mexico high desert sage
even the hummingbirds will buzz your presence

if I scuba dive and snorkel off Cozumel
and touch a Queen Angel and stroke a spotted eagle ray
there you are, breathing and bubbling along

if I hide in my cerebral mess and wallow in pain
and push away with hands and feet any incarnate love
or busy my life with work and finance and hobby

and distract myself with tweets and digital friends
there you are, grabbing hold of me in the now of awareness
in the being and the self-deception and the running

will I finally find peace from the one who haunts
who never lets go of the chase or the hand or truth
and if I cannot escape this unbearable holiness

will I ever submit to its infinite and infinitesimal reality
and float in its mysterious salt-water buoyancy
or will it kill me first, and I end up exactly there anyway

# Another Kind of Raising Up

*Lectionary 21 C*
Luke 13:10–17

*And just then there appeared a woman with a spirit that had crippled her for eighteen years. She was bent over and was quite unable to stand up straight. When Jesus saw her, he called her over and said, "Woman, you are set free from your ailment." When he laid his hands on her, immediately she stood up straight and began praising God. (Luke 13:11–13)*

stooped so only the beetles could see her face
stuck in fractured vertebrae downward posture
bone on bone and the cracking of movement
crooked humility like forced back labor

and then the raising the release the renewal
freedom to stand up and breathe deep in the lungs
strengthened in spine and spirit and looking everyone eye to eye
another one lifted up to dignity and now:

a free,
gracious,
thankful
bow

# Parable of the Dinner Party

*Lectionary 22 C*
Luke 14:1, 7–14

> *When he noticed how the guests chose the places of honor, he told them a parable. When you are invited by someone to a wedding banquet, do not sit down at the place of honor, in case someone more distinguished than you has been invited by your host; and the host who invited both of you may come and say to you, 'Give this person your place,' and then in disgrace you would start to take the lowest place. (Luke 14:7–9)*

She entered the party like a caped queen
her heels lifting herself up to thinner air
almost to where she wanted to be

she saw the table spread with boutique finery
charcuterie and artisanal cheeses and duck liver pate
red and white and bubbling wine for every course

she approached the gathering and saw on the far end
the out-of-fashioned, the rough handed and wrong spoken
the servants and migrants who picked the butter lettuce

on the near end she saw well-labeled suits
handbags with leather and metal clasps
that look of confidence in the eyes of the highly educated

she saw one chair near her with those of her kind
she sat and mingled and sipped wine and laughed controllably
and knew which fork to use for the appetizer

the host came and thanked her for taking
the seat at this end and assured her warm-voiced
that someday, she too, could join him at the other

# The Terms of Peace

*Lectionary 23 C*
Luke 14:25–33

*Or what king, going out to wage war against another king, will not sit
down first and consider whether he is able with ten thousand to oppose
the one who comes against him with twenty thousand? If he cannot,
then, while the other is still far away, he sends a delegation and asks for
the terms of peace. (Luke 14:31–32)*

A king was bored with jesters and galas and grovelers
and decided to wage war on Thursday after eggs for breakfast
his afternoon equestrian lesson and massage and a nap

And so he rounded up his 10,000 warriors and their armaments
and they marched and trotted out to the field of blood
and blew the horns and fired the warning shots and waited

Soon the neighbor king's army precision marched over the hill
they looked to be double the size, robust and fiery
their swords were hardened and their trebuchets tall

So the bored king sent a message and asked with regal manners
the terms for peace and the way back to the royal routine
and the other king with his warriors in full display commanded

you should have counted the cost of war before bugling
the price of peace is your complete surrender to me
give up your weapons and shields and machines and pride

So Jesus with your foolish king, costly war parable, what are
the terms of peace with you, or are there none except surrender
and you will cajole us into following no matter our resistance to courage

else we be left in our torpor thrones and remote controls
wondering why we were born slight and why we will die forgotten
and daydream about the greater good that might have been

# Watson and Crick and Moses and Us

*Lectionary 24 C*
Exodus 32:7–14

*But Moses implored the LORD his God, and said, "O LORD, why does*
*your wrath burn hot against your people, whom you brought out of the*
*land of Egypt with great power and with a mighty hand? Why should*
*the Egyptians say, 'It was with evil intent that he brought them out to*
*kill them in the mountains, and to consume them from the face of the*
*earth'? Turn from your fierce wrath; change your mind and do not bring*
*disaster on your people. Remember Abraham, Isaac, and Israel, your*
*servants, how you swore to them by your own self, saying to them, 'I will*
*multiply your descendants like the stars of heaven, and all this land that*
*I have promised I will give to your descendants, and they shall inherit*
*it forever.'" And the LORD changed his mind about the disaster that he*
*planned to bring on his people. (Exodus 32:11–14)*


Watson and Crick and Moses saw mystery like magi
somewhere within you and all enigmatic things
there is a holy of holies like an empty full space
around which even you turn and turn and return
when the world gets off-balance and wobbles
your mad divine passion burns into the red zone
and dangerous hums sing of disintegration
and one of us feels the heat and touches the edge
calling you to your better side with audacious pleas
and so you turn even more than we do

drawing us into your twisting ladder of mercy
joining us in a double helix of compassion
and we become together, holy and mundane alike
a genome of hope that our mad ends are your becoming

# Helium

*Lectionary 25 C*
Amos 8:4–7

*Hear this, you that trample on the needy, and bring to ruin the poor of the land, saying, "When will the new moon be over so that we may sell grain; and the sabbath, so that we may offer wheat for sale? We will make the ephah small and the shekel great, and practice deceit with false balances, buying the poor for silver and the needy for a pair of sandals, and selling the sweepings of the wheat." The LORD has sworn by the pride of Jacob: Surely I will never forget any of their deeds. (Amos 8:4–7)*

I am the woman who bought your swept up wheat
and fed my toddler dirt and chaff cereal
I bought your tainted formula with poison filler
I used my dwindling public food aid for your surplus milk
When the great rising comes and we lowly are lifted first
your eyes will widen white in panic as you stay grounded
rushing to shed your wealth like ballast as I and my children
float upward in our promised privileged freedom
and you will wonder if I of all proximal people
will let you grab my heel to become your helium balloon
and in my singing joy I give you my gracious motherly *yes*

# Numb

*Lectionary 26 C*
Luke 16:19–31

> *But Abraham said, 'Child, remember that during your lifetime you received your good things, and Lazarus in like manner evil things; but now he is comforted here, and you are in agony. (Luke 16:25)*

Abraham's bosom comforts
the fatherless, wounded weeping son
like a fired hearth, a stew,
and a slow, knowing drum beat at night

all the hurting, sore Lazaruses of the earth
will gather there free and
nuzzle him until the pain is taken up
into God's own welcoming bosom

but not so for those who lounge
on white leather couches clutching
red wine goblets, who do not know
how to mourn the global wail

not to grieve is a luxury for the numbed
and pharmacologically well-fed
their anesthetic blocking the pain
but also the divine comfort of their longing

so drink up believers the cup of suffering
eat the bread of crumbled brokenness
have your numbed souls cracked open again
let the cosmic sorrow drip into you and feel

# How Not to Be Thanked

*Lectionary 27 C*
Luke 17:5–10

> *Who among you would say to your slave who has just come in from
> plowing or tending sheep in the field, 'Come here at once and take your
> place at the table'? Would you not rather say to him, 'Prepare supper for
> me, put on your apron and serve me while I eat and drink; later you may
> eat and drink'? Do you thank the slave for doing what was commanded?
> So you also, when you have done all that you were ordered to do, say,
> 'We are worthless slaves; we have done only what we ought to have
> done!'" (Luke 17:7–10)*

We did these servant duties
the feedings and healings and knitting and praying
the giving and cooking and fixing and cleaning
and then we tied these obligatory faith tasks

to neoprene white weather balloons hydrogen-filled
launched them into the stratosphere and beyond
to see where the ghostly wind might take them
soaring over cities and oceans and stadiums and slums

we let them go from our slavish egos to became part of
the seasons and the cycles and the ways of the global organism
so they were no longer us or part of us and no longer
tied to our oxygen-weighted lungs and brains and blood

we imagined they might rise up to God and burst from glory
and fall back to earth and shower the love-dry human fields
with drips of kindness and drops of compassion
and our entire selves might rise and burst and praise

# Trickster Savior

*Lectionary 28 C*
Luke 17:11–19

> *When he saw them, he said to them, "Go and show yourselves to the priests." And as they went, they were made clean. Then one of them, when he saw that he was healed, turned back, praising God with a loud voice. He prostrated himself at Jesus' feet and thanked him. And he was a Samaritan. Then Jesus asked, "Were not ten made clean? But the other nine, where are they? (Luke 17:14–17)*

His hair the color of gasoline
his smile as wide as a wild coyote
unpredictable as an August tornado
he comes to play his saving tricks on us

He sends ten lepers to the priest for healing
wondering if any will make a u-turn when wonder strikes
doing exactly what he says is missing the point
but the trip wire for exposure of myopic seriousness

He frustrates the easy day with interruptions like cats
and watches our pressure gauges glide past red
he slips a nail under the new car tire
and waits for profanity to roll

Everyone knows there is a trickster among us
no one seems to remember that his cunning
is the way he lets us in on the joke of grace
and traps us with his playful, winsome befriending

# Limp

*Lectionary 29 C*
Genesis 32:22–31

*So Jacob called the place Peniel, saying, "For I have seen God face to face,
and yet my life is preserved." The sun rose upon him as he passed Penuel,
limping because of his hip. (Gen 32:30–31)*


Because I journeyed too close to the event horizon
Because I dreamed deeper than REM and hallucination
Because I half-nelsoned the mystery into self-revelation
Because I knew silence is not the only holy way

I limp with a hip socket struck by marvelous pain
I limp with an ego wounded and the wound a blessing
I limp a survivor from a close encounter with the other
I limp slower and wiser, purple-hearted from the battle

Unable to walk briskly away from the one hiding among us
Unable to dance on with a smooth sliding stroll
Unable to run tremulous from the infinite unknowable
Unable to resist the one who would rather have a wrangle

# The Dead

***All Saints Day***
Daniel 7:1–3, 15–18

*But the holy ones of the Most High shall receive the kingdom and possess
the kingdom forever — forever and ever." (Daniel 7:18)*

The dead do not walk and ravage flesh and trample
do not haunt us into mimicking their traditions
and repeating their creeds until our numb tongues
stop tasting spice and heat and sour and now

The dead do not sit impatient judging us from next Thursday
or from some ill-calculated millennial crashing horizon
wondering if we will ever figure it out and solve the puzzle
as well as they did in their spurt of energized entropy on earth

The dead sing to us their layered madrigals of mettle
that we will listen to their small triumphs of concrete love
and sympathize with their incarnate suffering without verdict
welcoming what shards of their wisdom survived modernity

These holy ones draw us into the future with silk string tugs
urging us to feel the gentle pull even now in this still and stuck day
swamping our hearts with this one mystery that floods us all
the finite bears the infinite, even their and our wrecked finitudes

So on this point the Bible is surely wrong about the future
that there will be no more tears in the holy city
their eyes water the river of life with joy overflowing
as they sit with us already sipping wine on the downtown shore

# Iron Pen

*Lectionary 32 C*
Job 19:23–27

> *O that my words were written down! O that they were inscribed in a book! O that with an iron pen and with lead they were engraved on a rock forever! (Job 19:23–24)*

If my words were acidic enough to etch a metal plate
I could weld it to a skyscraper antenna and each letter would soar

If my pen were iron and everything I wrote were inscribed
into the stone surface of this earth even after I'm beneath it

If the photons entering your eye just now could burn in this line
and your hippocampus would remember me after I'm forgettable

But nothing I author into the universe will survive the curve
of the earth around the sun more than a time or two beyond me

And none of my juxtapositions will remain juxtaposed but toppled
and every insight I have known will spill into the black coffee swirl of time

All that will endure of me is the infinite already in me groping to find a way
into the small portal of this day or your eye or some soul's wound

So let this liquid fountain pen or these soft flesh fingertips do their
    temporal work
and this erasable life rejoice in the one who writes me speechless and eternal

# Reign on Me

*Christ the King Sunday C*
Jeremiah 23:1–6

> *The days are surely coming, says the LORD, when I will raise up for*
> *David a righteous Branch, and he shall reign as king and deal wisely,*
> *and shall execute justice and righteousness in the land. In his days Judah*
> *will be saved and Israel will live in safety. And this is the name by which*
> *he will be called: "The LORD is our righteousness." (Jer 23:5–6)*

Sweet strong sovereign of mercy
interfering with all rulers and their ruins
crushing every hegemony with fierce peace
holding sway from commoner streets

gently ruining every strategic move I plotted
to start a coup and run my own country
with a self-appointed cabinet of narcissism
and my weakling high chair tyrant whine

you are the one arch reigning over us all
that does not crumble or fail or condescend
but kindly breaks what must be broken
and muscularly blesses what needs to be blessed

# Title Index

Abacus              38
About that Plucking Out the Eye Thing              102
Adam and Eve Again              19
Airstream              21
And He Took Them Up in His Arms              104
Another Kind of Raising Up              169
Aquavit              23
Architecture              43
Art of Reformation              110
Ascension              81
Ash Thursday              133
Automatic Earth              88

Calling All Jerks              106
Calling All Kings              115
Chef              13
Count the Stars              167

Deep and Terrifying Darkness in which Covenant Comes              137
Devouring Fire              17
Did You Dream Tonight              153
Do for Us Whatever We Ask              108

Ease of Mystery              158
Edges              15
Epiphany One Way or Another              124

Fluo•res•cence              57
Friending              79

Gaudete              122
Glory Comes in Love              152
God Stuck Her Tongue Out              156
God's Bathrobe              84

# Title Index

Gracious Ritual of Ashes   18
Grief on a Hallowed Eve   49
Groping   34

Have You Not Known, Grasshopper   66
Helium   176
Hidden Face   55
Hidden in Plain Sight   132
Hope Is a Blue Note   3
How Not to Be Thanked   179

If Jesus Were Blind   24
If Only We Had Better Options   94
Impatience for Imposters   29
In the Night   61
Institutionalized Jesus   86
Iron Pen   184
It Was a Good Day for God   40

Jesus and the Boys   100
Jesus Naked in a Sacred Circle   69
Jesus: Cardiologist   96

Kenosis   27

Lazarus Acrostic   112
Limp   182
Little Stranger Cakes   164
Living Jesus   146
Lose Yourself Along the Way   98

Magnifying Glass   123
Melt   63
Mimetic Jesus   145

Near and Far, I'm Afraid   168
New Moon over Emmaus   30
No Angel Came   59
Numb   177

Occupy Temple   71
Oh Boy Jeremiah   130
Oh, to Be as Bad as Paul   150
Oil and Wine   162
On Taking the Watery Plunge   126
Openings and Obfuscations   10
Order of St. Thomas   148

Outside Inside Out 14

Palm or Passion, Wave or Particle 143
Parable of the Dinner Party 170
Passiontide 75
Pentecost Spiked Punch 82

Quiet Dismissal 6

Ready to Party 45
Reign on Me 185
Rumors 114

Sacred Wound Lifted Up 72
Samuel Sleeping in the Temple 65
Sense of Wisdom 92
Sentinels 37
Show Us 33
Shuttered Doors and Detours 165
Signs and Wonders 32
Spikenard 141
Suspense 151
Sympathy for Lazarus 25
Sympathy for the Emperor at Christmastime 7

Tattoo 47
The Bread that Satisfies 91
The Dead 183
The Meaning of God 9
The Messenger 121
The Resurrection Theater of the Absurd 77
The Terms of Peace 172
The Third Yes 42
The Wanderer 135
The Widow and the Cross 113
This Advent 4
Today 128
Training to See Stars 62
Trickster Savior 181
Trinity Is a Poem 36

Unbearable Lightness of Myself 11
Unity Complex 155

Watson and Crick and Moses and Us 174
We Know Love by This 78
What Job Meant to Say Had He Girded Up His Loins 90

## Title Index

What to Do with Your One Grain of Wheat                73
When My Time Comes for Ashes and Dust                 67
When the Manna Ran Out                               140
Wild Man John                                         56
Worthy                                               160

You Are Late                                          51
You Said Meet You by the Fig Tree                    119
Yours Not Mine (Unless with Yours)                   139

# Scripture Index

## OLD TESTAMENT

### Genesis

| | |
|---|---|
| 1:1–5 | 63 |
| 2:15–17, 3:1–7 | 19 |
| 15:1–6 | 167 |
| 15:1–12, 17–18 | 137 |
| 18:1–10a | 164 |
| 32:22–31 | 182 |

### Exodus

| | |
|---|---|
| 24:12–18 | 17 |
| 32:7–14 | 174 |

### Leviticus

| | |
|---|---|
| 19:1–2, 9–18 | 15 |

### Deuteronomy

| | |
|---|---|
| 26:1–11 | 135 |

### Joshua

| | |
|---|---|
| 5:9–12 | 140 |

### First Samuel

| | |
|---|---|
| 3:1–10 | 65 |

### Job

| | |
|---|---|
| 19:23–27 | 184 |

| | |
|---|---|
| 38:1–11 | 90 |

### Psalms

| | |
|---|---|
| 51:1–17 | 67 |

### Proverbs

| | |
|---|---|
| 9:1–6 | 92 |

### Isaiah

| | |
|---|---|
| 2:1–5 | 3 |
| 6:1–8 | 84 |
| 11:1–10 | 4 |
| 40:21–31 | 66 |
| 49:1–7 | 11 |
| 55:1–9 | 139 |
| 61:1–4, 8–11 | 57 |
| 63:1–9 | 55 |

### Jeremiah

| | |
|---|---|
| 1:4–10 | 130 |
| 23:1–6 | 185 |
| 23:23–29 | 168 |
| 31:31–34 | 110 |

### Ezekiel

| | |
|---|---|
| 33:7–11 | 37 |

### Daniel

| | |
|---|---|
| 7:1–3, 15–18 | 183 |

## Joel

| | |
|---|---|
| 2:1–2, 12–17 | 18, 133 |

## Amos

| | |
|---|---|
| 8:4–7 | 176 |

## Malachi

| | |
|---|---|
| 3:1–4 | 121 |

# NEW TESTAMENT

## Matthew

| | |
|---|---|
| 1:18–25 | 6 |
| 2:1–12 | 62, 124 |
| 3:13–17 | 10 |
| 5:13–20 | 13 |
| 5:21–37 | 14 |
| 18:21–35 | 38 |
| 20:1–16 | 40 |
| 21:23–32 | 42 |
| 21:33–46 | 43 |
| 22:1–14 | 45 |
| 22:15–21 | 47 |
| 25:1–13 | 51 |

## Mark

| | |
|---|---|
| 1:1–8 | 56 |
| 1:9–15 | 69 |
| 3:20–35 | 86 |
| 4:26–34 | 88 |
| 7:1–8, 14–15, 21–23 | 96 |
| 8:27–38 | 98 |
| 9:30–37 | 100 |
| 9:38–50 | 102 |
| 10:2–16 | 104 |
| 10:17–31 | 106 |
| 10:35–45 | 108 |
| 12:38–44 | 113 |
| 13:1–8 | 114 |
| 14:1–15:47 | 75 |
| 16:1–8 | 77 |

## Luke

| | |
|---|---|
| 1:26–38 | 59 |
| 1:39–55 | 123 |
| 2:1–20 | 7, 61 |
| 3:15–17, 21–22 | 126 |
| 4:14–21 | 128 |
| 7:1–10 | 160 |
| 9:28–43 | 132 |
| 10:25–37 | 162 |
| 11:1–13 | 165 |
| 13:10–17 | 169 |
| 14:1, 7–14 | 170 |
| 14:25–33 | 172 |
| 16:19–31 | 177 |
| 17:5–10 | 179 |
| 17:11–19 | 181 |
| 21:25–36 | 119 |
| 22:14–23:56 | 143 |
| 24:1–12 | 146 |
| 24:13–35 | 30 |

## John

| | |
|---|---|
| 1:1–18 | 9 |
| 2:13–22 | 71 |
| 3:1–17 | 21 |
| 3:14–21 | 72 |
| 4:5–42 | 23 |
| 6:1–21 | 91 |
| 6:56–69 | 94 |
| 9:1–41 | 24 |
| 10:22–30 | 151 |
| 11:1–45 | 25 |
| 11:32–44 | 112 |
| 12:1–8 | 141 |
| 12:20–30 | 73 |
| 13:1–17, 31b–35 | 145 |
| 13:31–35 | 152 |
| 14:1–14 | 33 |
| 15:9–17 | 79 |
| 16:12–15 | 158 |
| 17:20–26 | 155 |
| 18:33–37 | 115 |
| 20:19–31 | 29, 148 |

## Acts

| | |
|---|---|
| 1:1–11 | 81 |
| 2:1–21 | 82, 156 |
| 2:42–47 | 32 |
| 9:1–6 | 150 |
| 17:22–31 | 34 |

## 2 Corinthians

| | |
|---|---|
| 13:11–13 | 36 |

## Philippians

| | |
|---|---|
| 2:5–11 | 27 |
| 4:4–7 | 122 |

## First John

| | |
|---|---|
| 3:16–24 | 78 |

## Revelation

| | |
|---|---|
| 7:9–17 | 49 |
| 21:10, 22–22:5 | 153 |

# Liturgical Index

| | | | |
|---|---|---|---|
| Advent 1 A | 3 | Easter 5 A | 33 |
| Advent 1 B | 55 | Easter 5 C | 152 |
| Advent 1 C | 119 | Easter 6 A | 34 |
| Advent 2 A | 4 | Easter 6 B | 79 |
| Advent 2 B | 56 | Easter 6 C | 153 |
| Advent 2 C | 121 | Easter 7 C | 155 |
| Advent 3 B | 57 | Epiphany of Our Lord | 62, 124 |
| Advent 3 C | 122 | | |
| Advent 4 A | 6 | Holy Trinity A | 36 |
| Advent 4 B | 59 | Holy Trinity B | 84 |
| Advent 4 C | 123 | Holy Trinity C | 158 |
| All Saints / All Souls | 49, 112, 183 | | |
| Ascension of Our Lord | 81 | Lectionary 2 A | 11 |
| Ash Wednesday | 18, 67, 133 | Lectionary 2 B | 65 |
| | | Lectionary 3 C | 128 |
| Baptism of Our Lord A | 10 | Lectionary 4 C | 130 |
| Baptism of Our Lord B | 63 | Lectionary 5 A | 13 |
| Baptism of Our Lord C | 126 | Lectionary 5 B | 66 |
| | | Lectionary 6 A | 14 |
| Christ the King Sunday B | 115 | Lectionary 7 A | 15 |
| Christ the King Sunday C | 185 | Lectionary 9 C | 160 |
| Christmas Eve | 7, 61 | Lectionary 10 B | 86 |
| Christmas 2 ABC | 9 | Lectionary 11 B | 88 |
| | | Lectionary 12 B | 90 |
| Easter Sunday B | 77 | Lectionary 15 C | 162 |
| Easter Sunday C | 146 | Lectionary 16 C | 164 |
| Easter 2 A | 29 | Lectionary 17 B | 91 |
| Easter 2 C | 148 | Lectionary 17 C | 165 |
| Easter 3 A | 30 | Lectionary 19 C | 167 |
| Easter 3 C | 150 | Lectionary 20 B | 92 |
| Easter 4 A | 32 | Lectionary 20 C | 168 |
| Easter 4 B | 78 | Lectionary 21 B | 94 |
| Easter 4 C | 151 | Lectionary 21 C | 169 |

| | | | |
|---|---|---|---|
| Lectionary 22 B | 96 | Lent 2 A | 21 |
| Lectionary 22 C | 170 | Lent 2 C | 137 |
| Lectionary 23 A | 37 | Lent 3 A | 23 |
| Lectionary 23 C | 172 | Lent 3 B | 71 |
| Lectionary 24 A | 38 | Lent 3 C | 139 |
| Lectionary 24 B | 98 | Lent 4 A | 24 |
| Lectionary 24 C | 174 | Lent 4 B | 72 |
| Lectionary 25 A | 40 | Lent 4 C | 140 |
| Lectionary 25 B | 100 | Lent 5 A | 25 |
| Lectionary 25 C | 176 | Lent 5 B | 73 |
| Lectionary 26 A | 42 | Lent 5 C | 141 |
| Lectionary 26 B | 102 | | |
| Lectionary 26 C | 177 | Maundy Thursday | 145 |
| Lectionary 27 A | 43 | | |
| Lectionary 27 B | 104 | Nativity of Our Lord | 7, 61 |
| Lectionary 27 C | 179 | | |
| Lectionary 28 A | 45 | Palm / Passion Sunday A | 27 |
| Lectionary 28 B | 106 | Palm / Passion Sunday B | 75 |
| Lectionary 28 C | 181 | Palm / Passion Sunday C | 143 |
| Lectionary 29 A | 47 | | |
| Lectionary 29 B | 108 | Pentecost B | 82 |
| Lectionary 29 C | 182 | Pentecost C | 156 |
| Lectionary 32 A | 51 | | |
| Lectionary 32 B | 113 | Reformation Sunday | 110 |
| Lectionary 32 C | 184 | | |
| Lectionary 33 B | 114 | Resurrection of Our Lord B | 77 |
| | | Resurrection of Our Lord C | 146 |
| Lent 1 A | 19 | | |
| Lent 1 C | 135 | Transfiguration A | 17 |
| Lent 1 B | 69 | Transfiguration C | 132 |